To Matt
with very [...].
Paul

Face to Face

FACE TO FACE

Therapy as Ethics

PAUL GORDON

Constable · London

First published in Great Britain 1999
by Constable and Company Limited
3 The Lanchesters, 162 Fulham Palace Road
London W6 9ER
Copyright © Paul Gordon 1999
ISBN 0 09 479160 0
The right of Paul Gordon to be identified as author
of this work has been asserted by him in accordance with
the Copyright, Designs and Patents Act 1988
Set in Linotron Sabon 10½ pt by
SetSystems Ltd, Saffron Walden, Essex
Printed in Great Britain by
St Edmundsbury Press Ltd
Bury St Edmunds, Suffolk

A CIP catalogue record for this book
is available from the British Library

For
Melissa

Wherever I speak from or in what particular
Voice, this is always a record of me in you.

W. S. Graham: 'Malcolm Mooney's Land'

Contents

Acknowledgements   9

Introduction   13

1 What's wrong with psychotherapy?   19

2 'Vigilant passivity to the call of the other':
therapy as ethics   46

3 Language, listening and dialogue:
the therapeutic conversation   63

4 Waiting, witnessing and naming   86

5 'A dwelling in the evening air': the place of therapy   103

6 'Speech for that unspoken': the poetics of therapy   118

7 Psychotherapy in the world   137

8 'Where in the waste is the wisdom?'   154

Notes   164

Permissions   185

Index   186

Acknowledgements

It is harder to live well for a day than it is to write a book.

Adam Mickiewicz

A book, like any other statement, is a contribution to a conversation and while it is, in the end, written by a particular person or persons, it emerges from, and owes its existence to all those who have taken part in the conversation. Beyond the text, as someone once said, there is always the context. This is a way of saying that I am only too aware of what I owe to all those with whom, over the years, I have talked about psychotherapy, including those who have taught me and those whom I have taught; those who have supervised my clinical work and those whom I have supervised; and my friends and colleagues in the world of psychotherapy, especially at the Philadelphia Association where Robin Cooper, Steve Gans and John Heaton all read parts of this book in draft and gave me the benefit of their thoughtfulness. I am grateful too to friends and colleagues at the Institute of Psychotherapy and Social Studies, especially Veronica Norburn, Sue Sünkel and the late Giora Doron, and at Open Door, the young people's psychotherapy service where I have worked for several years. Without all of them this book would not be what it is.

For reasons of confidentiality, among others, I do not quote from my clinical work, but every page of this book is informed by my experience with those whom I have seen in therapy. This book would have been impossible without them. They have my gratitude.

9

I owe a very particular and inestimable debt to Veronica
Norburn and Robin Cooper who, in their very different ways,
helped me to find a voice, to take up a place not only in the
conversation of psychotherapy, but in the conversation of the
world.

Not for the first time I have been fortunate in having had a
group of friends willing to give me their time and thought,
their criticism and disagreements, as well as encouragement
and praise, usually in just the right measure. I am deeply
indebted to Al Gordon, Tony O'Connor (one-time 'philosopher in residence' at Victoria Road), Val Richards, Cathy
Troupp and Bob Young for their thoughful engagement with
my work and, equally important, the gift of their friendship.

I could not have hoped for a more sympathetic and respectful editor than Carol O'Brien or a more attuned reader than
David Smail.

The final stage of writing this book was marked by great
sadness at the deaths of two men to whom, in vastly different
ways, I owe a great deal. My father, Stanley Gordon, died the
day after I finished the penultimate revision of the text. The
conversation of psychotherapy was not one with which he
was familiar but he appreciated, I think, my efforts in it and
he would, I hope, have been proud of this one. A few days
later I learned of the death of the psychoanalyst and social
theorist, Cornelius Castoriadis, whose thought, more than
that of any other single figure, had shaped my thinking for
more than half my life and is reflected in parts of this book.

This book is dedicated, in some return for her faith and
love during the past decade and more, to Melissa Benn, *il
miglior fabbro*. She did everything possible to enable me to
write it, ensuring I had the time, discussing ideas, criticising
drafts, thinking of the title and, above all, by believing in this
book as much as I did and, at crucial times, more than I
could. Our daughters, Hannah and Sarah, the paragons of
paradox, made the writing of this book more difficult than it

might otherwise have been, but in their own inimitable – and not so easily articulated – way, they also made it possible. No one could have hoped for an environment more facilitating.

Paul Gordon
April 1998

If you engage in travel, you will arrive.

Ibn Arabi, 1165–1240

And that is the great thing, to make oneself free of the schools and indeed of all schools.

Paul Cézanne

In the last twenty years, psychotherapy has developed both in theory and in practice in complex ways. And yet through all this tangled complexity and sometimes confusion it is impossible, in the words of Pasternak, 'not to fall ultimately as into heresy, into unheard of simplicity' ... The irreducible elements of a psychotherapy are a therapist, a patient and a regular and reliable time and place. But given these, it is not so easy for two people to meet.

R. D. Laing

12

Introduction

Some time ago, longer in fact than I care to remember, when the idea of this book was slowly taking shape, I found myself sitting in one of my favourite cafés in central London engrossed in a book. The book, however, was not about psychoanalysis or psychotherapy – I seemed to be reading such books increasingly rarely – but about architecture. I would be hard pressed to say just exactly what Paul Shepheard's *What is Architecture?: an essay on landscapes, buildings and machines*[1] was 'about', but it was clear to me that here was someone who cared passionately about his subject and who was mounting a vigorous defence of *his* conception of it. It was, as he put it, a defence in the spirit of such essays as Gertrude Stein's *What is English Literature?* and E. H. Carr's *What is History?*, both of which attempted to explain their subjects from particular understandings: ' "What is architecture?" is not the same question as "What should architecture be?" ' '.[2]

This book was written in the spirit of Shepheard's endeavour. Indeed, I was tempted to call it *What is Psychotherapy?* had it not been for the danger of misrepresentation and of annoying unsuspecting purchasers in search of a practical guide to the field. This is a personal account of what the practice and the challenge of psychotherapy means to me. I write as someone who is, like Paul Shepheard, committed to my vocation – and I do believe it *is* a vocation in that it is

13

something that, in some way, to some extent, we feel *called upon* to do – but who is by turns disturbed, angered, amused, bored or just simply uninterested by much of what is said, written and done in its name. While at fleeting moments, usually after some dull conference or predictable seminar, I have been tempted to give the whole thing up, the truth is that I believe in the practice of psychotherapy as a means of alleviating mental distress and suffering and as a force for good in our society, albeit a fairly modest one. (By psychotherapy I include not only psychotherapy in a strict sense, but in the wider sense of anything that might be considered therapeutic, regardless of the words used to describe it. I use the word psychotherapy therefore as a shorthand to cover counselling and other therapeutic endeavours, and the word therapist to include anyone doing therapeutic work.) But I believe too that psychotherapists urgently need to engage in a process of conscious renewal, a sceptical re-examination of what it is we are doing or think we are doing. I use the word sceptical deliberately for this book owes a great deal to the sceptical tradition within philosophy. This position has nothing to do with an extreme posturing found in some self-styled postmodernist circles that questions whether we can really know anything, whether there is any such thing as truth. (According to some extreme variants there is no objective truth – except, apparently, the statement that there is none.) The sceptical tradition that I draw upon is concerned with constantly questioning and self-questioning what we do know – or think we know – and how we come to know it, not in order to 'deconstruct' knowledge (whatever that might mean) but in the pursuit of truth. It includes writers as diverse as the originator of the modern essay form, Montaigne, and more recent philosophers such as Merleau-Ponty and Levinas. The sceptical theme runs through this book albeit under different names and I return to it more directly at the end.

This book was born out of two contexts, one personal, the

14

other political. For many years I have found it increasingly difficult to answer the often asked question, 'What kind of therapist are you?'. I am not a Freudian – except in the sense that we are all, to some extent, Freudian in that we cannot readily look at our world in a pre-Freudian manner, as though Freud had never existed. Nor am I a Kleinian and certainly not a Lacanian, but none of the other multitude of varieties either. Most psychotherapeutic theories and approaches have something to tell us; they offer different perspectives on something that is, after all, inexhaustible – the human subject. But too often this 'something' is inflated into a theoretical position, congealed into dogma, into total and totalising systems. And it is this to which I am opposed.

This book then is an attempt to answer that question – 'What kind of therapist?' – to articulate a position, a position that avoids dogma and sectarianism but at the same time tries to avoid an unsatisfactory, inconsistent and self-contradictory 'eclecticism' that can too often be the alternative.

But this book is more than just an attempt at a personal answer to a personal question. It would have to be in order to be justified. The question 'What kind of therapist are you?' is also a political question. It requires that one take up a particular position, both within the world of psychotherapy and within the wider world in which psychotherapy is situated. So this book is also a *political* undertaking. It is an attempt to answer the question 'What is the place of psychotherapy today?'. There was a time – how long ago it now seems – when the practice of psychotherapy was, or at least could be, conjoined to a radical politics, a politics concerned with social change. Those days have gone and psychotherapy has more and more withdrawn from an engagement with the social and political world and become more and more concerned with its own status, with securing its own place in the sun. I want to argue that psychotherapy, at least the kind of psychotherapy that I am talking about, while being inescapably concerned with the individual, is at the same time inescapably bound up with the social and political world which it inhabits.

The form of this book reflects its purpose. I am not concerned to offer a critique of different theories of psychotherapy – there is enough of that available already for those who want it. Nor am I concerned to add a concept or idea to the existing body of psychotherapeutic theory, in what I think of as the building blocks method of writing whereby the writer seems required to trace the history of ideas, usually starting with Freud, showing that he knows all the relevant literature, and ending up with his own minor (or, admittedly, not so minor) contribution which in turn will be acknowledged in the next book and so on. As Miss Jean Brodie put it, for those who like that sort of thing, that is the sort of thing they like. Rather, what follows is a series of thoughts and reflections, partly polemical, about the undertaking of psychotherapy which, as I have said, reflect my own understanding of the endeavour and which I hope can contribute to the renewal that I believe to be necessary.

'I have only assembled a bunch of other men's flowers,' Montaigne wrote, 'providing of my own only the string that binds them together.'[3] Given that so much has already been said, so much of value, and said so well, better than any possible paraphrase, in some respects this book may be read as a mosaic of other people's thoughts, other people, moreover, who are too little known, too infrequently encountered within the world of psychotherapy.

Before setting out my own position on the psychotherapeutic encounter a few words seem to me appropriate, necessary even, on the current state of psychotherapy and what seems to me to be wrong with it. This is what I do, in slightly polemical fashion, in Chapter 1. I am concerned here not with the more sensational kind of accusations made against psychotherapy and psychotherapists that one reads or hears about in the media such as dubious techniques of memory recovery or sexual or financial abuse. These – does it really need to be said? – are of course important and are to be dealt with accordingly. Rather I am concerned with what seems to me to be wrong with the *normal, accepted practices* of psychotherapy. These require our attention. In Chapter 2, drawing on the thinking of the French–Jewish philosopher Emmanuel Levinas, particularly around the idea of responsibility for the other, I draw the outlines of what I regard as an ethical psychotherapy, of psychotherapy *as* ethics. The rest of the book may be seen as an articulation of such an ethical psychotherapy, moving from the world of the consulting room to the world in which that room and all that takes place in it resides. Chapter 3 explores the parameters of the therapeutic conversation, at what happens when two people meet and talk, or try to. Chapter 4 continues this exploration, focusing on three therapeutic activities which are too little discussed – witnessing, waiting and naming. In Chapter 5 I look at the meaning of place in therapy, both the physical place in which therapy takes place and the metaphorical meanings of place. In Chapter 6 I look at the meaning of poetry and the poetic process and how these seem to me to be directly relevant to thinking about and doing psychotherapy. In Chapter 7 I locate psychotherapy in the world in which it is situated, arguing for a more engaged and socially reflective practice. In the last chapter I draw the outlines of a more sceptical, but nevertheless still committed, approach to psychotherapeutic thought and practice.

Psychotherapy, Peter Lomas has persuasively argued in a series of books, is a much more *ordinary* kind of relationship or encounter than we like to think.[4] But ordinary does not mean insignificant or unimportant. Think of the activities in a human life – cooking food, eating a meal, listening to music, reading a book, watching a film, meeting friends, making love, having sex, giving birth, rearing children, falling ill, getting old, dying. These are all perfectly ordinary things and every human being will do some of them at least at some time, but they are far from unimportant – although we may not give them much thought – and certainly not insignificant. They are life and what make us human and they are worthy of examination, of thought. 'Things are simple or complex according to how much attention is paid to them,' as Bernard MacLaverty puts it in *Grace Notes*.[5] So, what I am after is a return to the ordinary, to simplicity, but this must be a simplicity that is not simplistic. 'The simple expression of the complex thought' is how the painter Mark Rothko and his colleagues described what they sought in their art and anyone who has ever been moved by Rothko's work will know the meaning of this. They will know too the consummate craft involved in making what might seem at first looking to be simple slabs of colour into something that can move us, if we allow it, to the depths of our being. With all due modesty, this is what I am after, in the hope of contributing something to the renewal of psychotherapy that I believe to be necessary.

1

What's wrong
with psychotherapy?

*The real problem for the therapist is being a
therapist.*

David Cooper[1]

*Discretion is thus incompatible with a good pres-
entation of psychoanalysis. One has to become a
bad fellow, transcend the rules, sacrifice oneself,
betray, and behave like the artist who buys paints
with his wife's household money, or burns the
furniture to warm the room for his model. Without some such criminality there is no real
achievement.*

Sigmund Freud[2]

In one of Raymond Carver's short stories a cardiac surgeon
is telling some friends about an elderly couple who have been
in a serious car crash. Both husband and wife are severely
injured although it is clear that they will survive. What most
upsets the husband, the surgeon says, is not his injuries but
that, because of all his bandages, he is unable to see his wife.
And yet we talk, the surgeon protests to his friends, as if we
know what it is we talk about when we talk about love.[3] So
too, it seems to me, we talk as though we *know* what it is we
talk about when we talk of psychotherapy. We can hear and

19

read a lot about what supposedly happens in the course of psychotherapy. But too often we encounter, not humility and thoughtfulness in the face of human complexity and suffering, but rather an arrogance, a 'will to power' on the part of the therapist, a posturing that it is she who *really knows* what is going on. Frequently, too, patients are presented in terms that are not far from judgemental, loaded with (implicit) moralising baggage.

It is impossible to pretend that everything in the garden of psychotherapy is lovely. Yet what is wrong is not so much, as I suggested in the introduction, what is so often said in the mass media, criticism that is often driven by ignorance and cheap sensationalism and the critic's fear of what therapy represents – the irrational and unruly world of the emotions and passions. It is not so much that we engage in the abuse of those who seek our help, as is so often alleged. (If we were to believe popular discourse there are times one could be forgiven for thinking that all psychotherapists, when they are not actually engaged in sexual relations with their patients, are planting false memories of sexual abuse or just taking gross financial advantage of them.) Where these things happen, of course, it goes without saying, it is a serious matter and must be dealt with appropriately. It is not that everything is fine but that what is wrong is something other than what most public critics claim. This something, moreover, is much more widespread and consequently much more harmful, at least potentially, than the occasional individual case of abuse. It is to be found in our attitudes to our work and to the world in which we work, both as individuals and as a profession.

THE ODOUR OF SANCTIMONY

It is impossible to move in the world of psychotherapy for any length of time without encountering one of its most unpleasant characteristics – sanctimoniousness. The dictionary says that sanctimonious means 'making a show of sanctity or piety'; sanctity invokes not only saintliness but also the 'odour of sanctity', which refers to a reputation for holiness and derives from the sweet odour apparently exhaled by the dying or exhumed saint.

All this seems to me pretty appropriate for there is – or at least can be – a rather suffocating religious odour about the world of psychotherapy. One can sense it when one steps into the very buildings of psychotherapy organisations. It can be there whenever a group of psychotherapists are gathered together. It can be in the journals and books. And of course the parallels with religion are not hard to find: we have our holy books or texts (the Standard Edition of Freud, the Collected Works of Jung, the papers of Winnicott, the Seminars of Lacan and so on); we have our sanctified figures, too many to mention but every psychotherapy organisation or school seems to have one; we have sects in abundance and, of course, a good deal of sectarianism; and we have our own lines of apostolic succession – of who analysed whom, who saw whom for therapy, and who supervised whom – who is therefore among the elect, the chosen.

Some of this sanctimony derives from the idea that psychotherapy is part of that dreadful constellation, 'the caring professions'. But caring is not what psychotherapy is or should be about. It is not that I don't care about those I see in therapy; of course I do, but I do so in a very particular way. I am not involved in the *business* of caring, a business which is, or certainly can be, patronising and infantilising and which usually involves some notion of how the recipient of

21

care *should* be. This, of course, is defined by the professional. What we, as psychotherapists, are or should be involved in is something different. It is, as I shall argue in the rest of this book, about responsibility, which has nothing to do with care, at least in the way that this word has, sadly, come to be used. If psychotherapy needs a motto, Robin Cooper has suggested, it might be 'At least we don't care.'[4] Alternatively we might adopt Eliot's line, 'Teach us to care and not to care'.

Part of this sanctimoniousness is a humourlessness, a fear of being amused, of laughing in our work even though much of what we hear in the course of it is funny. 'I wonder,' the great psychoanalyst W. R. Bion once asked, 'if it is within the rules of psychoanalysis to be able to laugh at ourselves? Is it according to the rules of psychoanalysis that we should be amused and find things funny? Is it permissible to enjoy a psychoanalytic meeting?'[5] Perhaps we are afraid of being thought not serious, of being frivolous or even callous, or worst of all perhaps, of colluding with the patient's defences. We have to be so serious all the time. This is not to argue for the incorporation of humour into some supposed psychotherapeutic technique, as a sort of tool or strategy. Nothing could be more depressing in this context than to come across the inevitable book from an American psychoanalytic publisher on 'The use of humour in the psychoanalytic session'. Humour, need it be said, cannot be roped into service in this way.

This humourlessness is part of something broader. It reflects a particular attitude to our work. If being a therapist is as arduous, as difficult and as free of enjoyment as many of those who write about it suggest, why on earth, asks Peter Lomas, do we do it? We are easily drawn, he remarks, into the 'heroic yet narcissistic attractions of pain and sacrifice', and there is little talk of the enjoyment and fun in the therapeutic relationship. Even Winnicott, Lomas writes, 'who had such a childlike sense of fun in conversation, surprisingly writes as if his work demanded such a degree of patience, stoicism and subjugation of his own needs that it required a valiant effort beyond the ordinary.'[6] And what does it say about the nature of our work and our attitude to those we see, if this is the spirit in which we approach it? Do we really only *survive* as psychotherapists, as Nina Coltart suggested in the title of one of her books? If we were to break through in this 'revolutionary matter of being amused in the sacred process' of psychotherapy, Bion went on, we could see where this more joyous state took us.

THE ARROGANCE OF THERAPEUTIC POWER

Caring, at least of the kind I am speaking of, appears to be humble yet is anything but. To the contrary it stems from an arrogance, the arrogance of knowledge and power – or at least assumed knowledge. For the carer *knows* what is wrong with the other, knows what the other needs, better of course than she herself, and has the power to do something about it. (I doubt that I am the only one who cringes with embarrassment at the public suggestion of 'counselling' for almost anyone nowadays who finds themselves in some traumatic state, whether this be a lone sailor trapped in an upturned boat for days, or those caught up in some terrible accident.)

This arrogance isn't just about caring, however. It's something much much wider and may be inherent in the theory and practice, certainly of psychoanalysis, if not of other forms of therapy too. Where therapy is based on the idea that there is something troubling the patient that she does not know about but the therapist does, the field is ripe for the kind of arrogance I am talking about. (We see this whenever we hear therapists say that they 'showed' the client something; 'showed' the client her envy, her narcissism and so on.)

Now many people will respond that therapy is a shared endeavour, in which therapist and client together are involved in looking for meaning and understanding. But all too often this is not what happens. The therapist, despite denials, is the one who *knows* what is going on. After all, she has read the books, she knows the theory, she has been *trained*, and nowadays, what's more, she is registered and has a certificate to prove it. Even those who chant the Lacanian mantra of 'the subject who is supposed to know', of which mystification the patient is supposed to be disabused in the course of analysis, or who cite Foucault's critiques of knowledge and power, many of them, in their heart of hearts, know.

This arrogance is not just something that exists between the therapist and client. It is to be found also in the intolerance and sectarianism evident within the profession of psychotherapy. The history of psychoanalysis, for example, is a history rivalling that of the political far left in its splits, sectarianism, in-fighting, doctrinal disputes, paranoia and general unpleasantness and bad behaviour. It is a history in which, for instance, Freud's biographer Ernest Jones sought to characterise Freud's one-time colleague Ferenczi as psychotic; R. D. Laing, it is averred *sotto voce*, was psychotic; and critics from within are dismissed, whether formally as in the cases of Reich and Lacan, who were both expelled from the International Psycho-Analytic Association, or informally with the frequently heard 'She has not been properly trained/ analysed' to which, of course, there is no rejoinder. (Charles Rycroft recalled how Melanie Klein even said this to him in public when he questioned her theories.[7])

So too we have the spectacle of the psychoanalytic establishment fighting to maintain its arrogated copyright on the term 'psychoanalysis', even to the extent of writing to newspapers to 'warn' the public about others – not of their ilk – daring to call themselves 'psychoanalysts'. (In one recent case the (Lacanian) Centre for Freudian Analysis and Research had advertised a conference in the *London Review of Books* only to elicit a letter from the Institute of Psycho-Analysis saying that there was 'acceptance' within the mental health world that the term 'psychoanalyst' referred to someone trained by the British Psycho-Analytical Society or another component of the International Psycho-Analytic Association. The Lacanians, of course, are outside such bodies.) In this respect, psychoanalysis stands apart from other disciplines, for example physics or philosophy, where there may well be fierce and bitter disputes but where the accusation that 'something is not physics or philosophy' is not made, when it is not uncommon to hear it said of another position that 'it is not psychoanalysis'.[8]

From within the belly of the beast, so to speak, we have the observations of the prominent British psychoanalyst Nina Coltart who wrote late in her life of the 'fanaticism bordering on the religious' found within the British Psycho-Analytical Society, where people who disagree are frequently said to be not properly trained or not doing 'real analysis'.[9] From the other side of the Atlantic, the American analyst Kenneth Eisold has written recently on what he calls the intolerance of diversity found within psychoanalytic institutes. Eisold attributes this not just to the nature of the work – which is isolated and demanding – and to the nature of the institutes themselves which he describes as 'overbounded', that is rigid, impermeable and inflexible, but to an arrogant rejection of the outside world, a rejection which began with Freud and his followers and which is seen today in the privileged sense of immunity felt from the ambition, envy, competition and turbulence of the world.[10]

Of course, the world of psychoanalysis is not the world of psychotherapy, only a small part of it. Yet it is an important part, having much influence. It does not, in any case, stand alone in the world of psychotherapy in its intolerance.

THE WILL TO SCIENCE

A further problem with psychotherapy is the desire, the drive to be thought 'scientific'. Of course, psychotherapists want to be taken seriously; it would be strange if we did not. But there is also a desire for a certain standing or status and that's a different matter. Nowhere is this anxiety about status more evident than in the debate about whether psychotherapy is or is not scientific.

It is sometimes said that whether or not psychotherapy is a science is a debate of the past. Now, supposedly, we are content (or should be) to see psychotherapy as being about the construction of narratives, or a form of interpretation, or a matter of hermeneutics or whatever. And yet the claim to science persists. Psychoanalysis 'aims at being the science of the human mind,' claims one of the most prominent contemporary psychoanalysts, Hanna Segal,[11] while one popular and respected textbook carries the title, *Individual Psychotherapy and the Science of Psychodynamics*. So too many psychotherapy organisations insist on having their 'scientific meetings' at which people present 'scientific papers'. Underlying much of the discussion on this matter is an anxiety, an anxiety that if we are not scientific then we must be the opposite, unscientific, and it is from this that we psychotherapists want to distinguish ourselves – the world of faith healers, shamans, witch doctors, astrologists. We want to associate with other scientific spirits like medical doctors.

Like so much else in our discipline this preoccupation with the scientific began with Freud, not only in his much-quoted wish that psychoanalysis would eventually find a basis in neurology and physiology, but in many other remarks in which he sought to ally psychoanalysis to the natural sciences. This desire to be thought scientific also affected Freud's translators who, according to Bruno Bettelheim, substituted

pseudo-scientific neologisms (id, ego and super ego, for
instance, along with dreadful inventions like cathexis, para-
praxis and others) for the everyday German of the original:
'Instead of instilling a deep feeling for what is most human in
all of us, the translations attempt to lure the reader into
developing a "scientific" attitude toward man and his actions,
a "scientific" understanding of the unconscious and how it
conditions much of our behaviour.'[12]

However, Freud did not invent or develop a science but
rather, as Wittgenstein maintained, 'a manner of speaking'.
This was not an arbitrary construction, rather 'something
inventive and ingenious . . . a new system of expression', but
nevertheless not a scientific theory. A problem arises only
where a systematic confusion is revealed between science,
which must be subject to empirical control, and the imaginative activity of inventing a system of notation.[13] 'Freud is
constantly claiming to be scientific. But what he gives is
speculation – something prior even to the formation of a
hypothesis.'[14]

The notion of science employed by most of those involved
in discussions about the nature of psychotherapist and scien-
tist, Joe Schwarz reminds us, is pretty far removed from what
science actually means. Schwarz argues that people tend to
have a highly idealised view of what science is and what goes
on in it: we think evidence is offered, the participants look at
it and – presto! – a new paradigm comes into being. One of
the functions served by this view is to present and preserve
science in its role as an unchallengeable voice of authority.
The problem is that this notion of science as objective, precise
and above all *certain*, is mythic science, not real. Against this,
Schwarz cites the remark of the physicist Max Planck who
recalled that the most important fact he had learned from a
bitter dispute fifty years earlier was that a new scientific truth
does not triumph by convincing its opponents and making
them see the light, but rather because its opponents gradually

die off and a new generation grows up that is familiar with it.[15] So too the French psychoanalyst and social theorist Cornelius Castoriadis argued that contrary to prevailing common-sense ideas, science is fraught with riddles and unsolvable problems, including even the 'hardest' of sciences, mathematics and physics.[16]

As the philosopher of science Paul Feyerabend was always saying, in the world of scientific investigation and research, the truth is that anything goes – and has done – and the notion of some objective and principled scientific method is very far from the truth. He opened his (in)famous book *Against Method* with the following remark:

> The idea of a method that contains firm, unchanging, and absolutely binding principles for conducting the business of science meets considerable difficulty when confronted with the results of historical research . . . there is not a single rule, however plausible, and however firmly grounded in epistemology, that is not violated at some time or other . . . such violations are not accidental events, they are not the results of insufficient knowledge or of inattention which might have been avoided. On the contrary, we see that they are necessary for progress. Indeed, one of the most striking features of recent discussions in the history and philosophy of science is the realisation that events and developments, such as the invention of atomism in antiquity, the Copernican Revolution, the rise of modern atomism . . . the gradual emergence of the theory of light, occurred only because some thinkers either *decided* not to be bound by certain 'obvious' methodological rules, or because they *unwittingly broke* them.[17]

While it is good to be reminded of the truth as opposed to the myth of science, this can still lead us into thinking that psychotherapy is scientific, since what is being suggested is a more flexible notion of the scientific into which psycho-therapy might more easily fit. But psychotherapy isn't a science in any meaningful sense of the term. If it were we should be able to predict outcomes of treatment to some reasonable extent, taking account of such 'variables' as the nature of the problem, the type of therapy, the time available and so on. But of course we cannot. Nor should we be concerned about this. The terms of the debate are misguided. Not being scientific does not mean we are unscientific but, rather, that we are involved in something else altogether. Painting is not a science, writing is not a science, cooking is not a science, but it would be meaningless to describe them as 'unscientific'. They are rather endeavours *sui generis*, cre-ative, arts and crafts, which require their own disciplines and operate according to their own rules and conventions.

So why then does the debate go on? This constant recourse to the idea of the scientific seems, as I have said, to be part of a longing or search for status, a wish to be taken seriously and to put a distance between psychotherapy and the 'unscientific'.

A more honourable argument is that in an era of scarce resources for public funding of psychotherapy services, psychotherapy needs to be able to come up with evidence that it has some efficacy. But does this inevitably mean what has come to be called 'empirical psychoanalysis', complete not only with graphs, Venn diagrams and the like, but the attempted measuring of human behaviour and attitudes as in the worst of objectifying psychology? Is this what psycho-therapy is coming to? While it is true that those working in the public sector or otherwise dependent on public funds do have to account for their work, this does not have to be done in this way. Indeed, in a society where the consumer is supposed to be sovereign, one might expect that the con-sumers of psychotherapy be asked what they think. This of course rarely happens. Indeed, to the contrary, what people think and feel about their own experiences of therapy is dismissed as subjective.

THE (PSEUDO)MEDICALISATION OF THERAPY

One of the consequences of the increasing professionalisation of psychotherapy is a tendency, in some circles at least, to ape the medical profession and the medical model of the mind. This, of course, is not a new development; it has existed since psychotherapy began, but it does seem to have become more widespread. This is evident in the pseudo-medical language used by many psychotherapists – people engage in treatment, psychotherapists make diagnoses, people have symptons, suffer from delusions, obsessive compulsive disorder, borderline personality disorder or whatever. (In Stephen Poliakoff's play *Sweet Panic*, Mrs Trevell, the anxious mother – played in the production I saw by the marvellous Saskia Reeves – amuses herself by inventing psychological jargon, my own favourite being 'traumatic overhang'.) Even the word patient – while in a sense the most accurate word for those in therapy as someone who endures or suffers – seems to me favoured in order to boost medical pretensions. Is it only a matter of time, I wonder, before we are issued with white coats along with our registration certificates?

There is also a regrettable tendency among some psychotherapists to engage in (almost) routine contact with the GPs of people who consult them. What has happened, I wonder, to the idea of the psychotherapeutic space as a private, confidential and privileged arena where two people may explore, or at least attempt to explore, the difficulties that one is facing, free from external interference? We can, of course, see this as well-meaning and motivated by concern for one's patients. It can be understood at times in terms of the inexperienced therapist's anxiety, the need to share the burden of treatment, and in particular as a sort of insurance policy if things start to go seriously wrong, if for instance a patient becomes suicidal or is engaging in dangerous behaviour. (There is, I believe, a great deal of confusion in any case among therapists about our legal responsibility.) Nevertheless, once one begins to contact third parties then the therapy has become compromised or at least is in danger of becoming so.

The danger to the independence of psychotherapy is, at times, no more evident than in its relationship to the world of psychiatry. Somewhere in his writings, Freud expressed his concern that psychoanalysis would become 'a handmaiden to psychiatry' – that is, that it would lose its independence. To a significant extent this is just what has happened. Psychotherapy has to a marked degree lost or seriously compromised its independent standing. We do well to remind ourselves that Freud wrote his 1926 polemic *The Question of Lay Analysis* as a defence of Theodor Reik, the Austrian psychoanalyst who was not medically qualified and who had been charged with quackery in the United States. And Freud was clear in his desire to keep psychoanalysis apart from psychiatry although he was to find himself with serious opposition among his followers, especially in the United States.

The critique of psychiatry articulated by R. D. Laing, David Cooper, Felix Guatarri, David Ingleby and others in the 1960s and 1970s has become not just history, but forgotten history, subjected to that process of 'social amnesia' that Russell Jacoby has described, a process of forgetting that is concerned only with what is new. Recent contributions to this debate, for example Peter Breggin's *Toxic Psychiatry*, seem hardly known in the world of psychotherapy.

But has psychiatry changed in the thirty years since David Cooper wrote *Psychiatry and Anti-Psychiatry*? No doubt it has and no doubt too it has changed at least in part in response to the challenges of the anti- and critical psychiatrists, however much orthodox psychiatry might deny this. But it has not changed *fundamentally*. Despite the closure of the large psychiatric hospitals and the advent of the grossly misnamed policy of 'care in the community', psychiatrists continue to wield considerable power – to detain people, to carry out ECT, to force medication. Indeed, it might be argued that the power of psychiatry has increased precisely because of the dispersal of those designated mentally ill and the advent of 'community psychiatry'. The power of psychiatry has become less concentrated but more penetrative.

But it is not just a question of psychiatrists. It is about the nature of psychiatry, as the anti- and critical psychiatrists always maintained. While some psychiatry has undoubtedly become more social in its thinking, some has undoubtedly become more organic and physical, even more than it was already, believing the causes of disorders and distress to lie in chemical imbalances. The critiques of the anti- and critical psychiatrists remain valid. Objective psychiatry, Laing said, is an unobjective attempt to control largely non-objective events by objective means.[18] Psychiatry is the only branch of medicine which treats biologically conditions for which there is little or no biological evidence. Similarly David Cooper noted that psychiatrists got lost in the intricacies of organic medicine: 'They gradually and painstakingly acquire a requisite ignorance concerning the other person (patient) whom they confront or, more usually, refuse to confront'.[19]

Supposed advances in psychiatry have not brought to an end some of the even more barbaric practices. It was always salutary to arrive at the large hospital where I once saw outpatients for psychotherapy and be greeted each week by the notice on the ground floor of the brand new building where the psychotherapy department was located. There was an arrow pointing one way to 'Psychotherapy' and an arrow pointing the other way to 'ECT'.

So too should we be less starry-eyed or even just compla-
cent about the so-called advances in drug treatment in psychiatry. While such drug treatments have made significant
inroads into the management of mental illness, that is all they
are doing – managing. They are not curing. And to dismiss
the conditions that such treatments bring about – severe
weight gain, uncontrollable, Parkinsonism-like movements, a
numbing of the emotions and so on – as 'side effects' is not
only to play down the awfulness of these direct consequences;
it is also, as Oliver Sacks has remarked, to divide the world
into arbitrary bits and deny the reality of an organised whole.

It is not a question of being for or against psychiatry,
whatever that might mean, but of working out the relationship of psychiatry to psychotherapy and, above all, of maintaining a critical position in relation to both.

THE LURE OF PROFESSIONALISM

So used are we to speaking of professionalism as a compli-
ment that it may seem bizarre to criticise psychotherapy for
seeking to become a profession. We speak of someone as
'thoroughly professional' and it is a sign of approval; if,
conversely, we describe someone as unprofessional it's a
criticism and quite a serious one. And yet things are not quite
that straightforward. Let us recall the critique of professionalism by Ivan Illich in a series of books written only twenty
or so years ago but now scarcely referred to. In books such
as *Deschooling Society* and *Medical Nemesis*, Illich called
into question the common-sense view that medicine, education and other so-called advances in knowledge had been
unqualified benefits to society. Indeed, Illich claimed, they
acted against the interests and potentials of those they were
supposed to help. Schooling taught one little of real value,
stifled real learning and creativity and induced, or attempted

33

to induce, habits of obedience; organised medicine produced illness as much as it cured anything.

Our time, Illich suggested, should be called 'The age of disabling professions', an age when people had problems, experts had solutions, and scientists measured imponderables such as abilities and needs. While all trade associations attempt to determine how particular work shall be done and by whom, professions go further. They have the power to decide *what* shall be made and for whom, and how their decrees shall be enforced. They *tell* us what we need and claim the power to describe it. Indeed the true mark of the professional is precisely the authority to define someone as a client, to determine that person's need and to prescribe the appropriate treatment. The professionals assert secret knowledge about human nature, knowledge which only they have the power to dispense. The bodies of the twentieth-century professional specialist, Illich claimed, are more deeply entrenched than a Byzantine bureaucracy, endowed with wider competencies than any shaman, and equipped with a tighter hold over those they claim as victims than any Mafia.[20]

As for the layperson, she is turned into a passive, docile recipient whose world is an 'echo chamber of needs'. The client of the professional, one of Illich's co-authors, John McKnight, remarks, isn't so much someone who has needs as someone who *is needed*. She is less a consumer than the raw material for the servicing system; both input and output, her function is to meet the needs of servicers, the servicing system and the national economy.[21]

While it is true that psychotherapy has not proceeded as far in its development as a profession as say, medicine, law or social work, it is now headed well down that road. Psychotherapy now has its own professional register – indeed in the world of British psychoanalytic psychotherapy there are two competing registers; there are professional standards in the form of so-called codes of ethics; therapists are required to have professional insurance; trainings have become more externally regulated and are increasingly linked to the world of formal education.

Such developments, it is often said, protect the public. But this is questionable. There is at least a tendency – one might even go so far as to call it a law like Robert Michel's,'iron law of oligarchy' which stipulated that all political organisations degenerate in an anti-democratic manner – that professions exist or come to exist to protect their own members first. They become, George Bernard Shaw said, conspiracies against the public. Anyone who has ever tried to make a formal complaint or seek redress from a lawyer or doctor will know the meaning of this.

It is far from obvious that professionalism will lead to better standards of psychotherapeutic work. While it is reasonable to expect a solicitor to know and understand the basic laws of the land, or a doctor to be able to recognise and offer appropriate treatment for common ailments and illnesses, psychotherapy is nothing of this kind. We are not in the business of diagnosis or treatment and because the medical or objective model of the person does not apply to what we do, the objective model of recourse does not seem relevant either. We are engaged in a particular type of conversation with those we see in a mutual attempt to understand their difficulties in living their lives. This is what makes external regulation of psychotherapy so very difficult. A conversation that makes sense to some can seem absurd to others. It would be a strange and horrible world if certain kinds of conversation were to be controlled or even prohibited.

As for codes of ethics to which all therapists are required to adhere, it may seem as if these are a 'good idea' but they do little or nothing to protect the public. They tell us nothing, surely, that we do not accept for ourselves as a result of how we understand the process of psychotherapy. As a psychotherapist I do not need a code of ethics to tell me not to exploit someone financially or to give adequate notice of any absence or termination. Nor do I need a code of ethics to tell me I should not engage in sexual relations with patients. I do not do this because of my own personal ethics and because of my understanding of transference and of the power relationship between therapist and patient, of what takes place in the therapy.

This, of course, is not a sufficient argument against such codes, which are after all laying down minimal standards and which may, as is sometimes said, protect particularly vulnerable members of the public from unscrupulous practitioners. The danger lies in the bureaucratisation of psychotherapy. Is it really fanciful to envisage a future involving much greater external standardisation of training, restrictions on the kinds of therapy one may or may not offer, and generally greater interference in what till now has been a relatively free and independent movement? It is already possible to see that formal complaints procedures are encouraging complaints to be made, rather than be discussed within the therapy, while compulsory professional insurance is encouraging more legal actions against therapists by disgruntled and dissatisfied patients. And while we may be content for the moment to agree that sexual relations between psychotherapist and patient are unethical, in California, according to Susie Orbach, licensed psychotherapists are *required* to hand to every patient a leaflet which boldly states, 'Sex is always wrong.'[22] The mind boggles at the effect this must have on the person entering therapy, at the messages it is sending out. Is this where we are headed?

Psychotherapists are being caught in a trap of our own making. In seeking greater professional status and recognition we are subjecting ourselves to more and more constraints and in doing so run the risk of losing our independence of thought and action, which is necessary if psychotherapy is to be free, if we are to maintain that stance of indiscretion and criminal-

ity that Freud himself maintained was necessary for psychotherapy to flourish.

THE TYRANNY OF THEORY

> *Now gode. Let us leave theories there and return*
> *to here's here.*
>
> James Joyce[23]

In discussions about therapy, theories, supposedly used to
understand and explain what happens in psychotherapy,
became ever more elaborate. But whether they are at all
necessary or indeed helpful does not seem to be asked. After
all, what is happening? Two people meet in a room and talk
– or not. It is, Bion once remarked, absurdly simple and yet
'so simple that it is hard to believe how difficult it is.'[24] Too
often the theories just prevent us seeing what is before us, this
simple fact in all its complexity.

We suffer, Bion said on another occasion, from an indiges-
tion of theories, 'until it is almost impossible to hear what the
patient says. The trouble today is not ignorance of psychoanalytic theories; the trouble is so many theories that you
cannot see the patient for them.'[25] 'We do not need theories,'
R. D. Laing similarly said, 'so much as the experience that is
the source of the theory.'[26]

Given our way of being in the world it is hard to imagine
we could do without theories; we use them all the time, even
when we do not think we are doing so. The notion of 'being
in the world', for instance, is a theoretical one, or at least one
based on presuppositions and ideas that must, if needs be, be
theorised. And yet as the remarks of Bion and Laing indicate,
the danger in therapy is that adherence to the theory gets in
the way, not only of seeing what is before us, but of actually
being with the other person. Theory leads us to think that we

37

know things, that we understand, and while it can be a useful support in difficult times, helping us to think about a particular person or problem, all too often it is a distraction and a flight from the difficulties of uncertainty and from not knowing. It can become, as the historian E. P. Thompson remarked, a set of 'abbreviated categories which too often close enquiry before it has commenced'.[27] In this respect, I recall someone who used to speak in clinical discussions as someone having a 'minus-K mother' – referring to Bion's schema – as though this actually meant anything.

A common example of a theoretical construct which gets in the way of seeing and being with another is that of the 'inner world' or 'internal reality'. '[W]e live in an internal world which is as real a place to live as the outside world . . .' as the distinguished post-Kleinian Donald Meltzer has put it.[28] But let us ask the simple question: Where is this 'inner world'? I cannot see it, I cannot touch it, I cannot show it to anyone else. This, of course, could be said of the mind also. But the concept of mind, too, is one that is taken too much for granted within the world of psychotherapy.

Now, it may be said that to talk of the 'inner world' is 'only' a manner of speaking, but manners of speaking not only *reflect* how we think (or how some people think) but *influence* how we think. While it may well be useful for some people to think in terms of 'theatres of the mind', for example, to borrow Joyce McDougall's phrase, the danger is that metaphor is taken for reality and becomes a fact, as indeed the quotation from Meltzer above makes clear. For him the 'internal world' is *as real* as the outside world. (Meltzer himself has taken this to new heights – or depths – with his notion of people who 'inhabit' particular regions of the body of the 'internal mother', notably the claustrum or rectal compartment.) As Susan Sontag has commented, one cannot think without metaphors, but that does not mean that

38

there are not some metaphors we might well abstain from or try to retire from working use.[29]

The truth is that there is no internal world or inner reality that is not an imaginative construct. This is not to deny that we have conversations with ourselves, that we think, ruminate and fantasise. This would be absurd. But the postulation of an 'inner world' is, as Wittgenstein said, a picture of the mind. Our thoughts and feelings do not lie in some inner world hidden or waiting to be expressed.

There is no inner man, as Merleau-Ponty puts it in the opening pages of *Phenomenology of Perception*, 'man is in the world, and only in the world does he know himself'. When I return to myself, Merleau-Ponty continues, from an excursion into the realm of dogmatic common sense or of science, 'I do not find a source of intrinsic truth, but a subject destined to the world.'[30] Accepting the Freudian idea that there are sexual symptoms at the root of all neuroses, Merleau-Ponty nevertheless argues that these symptoms symbolise a whole attitude, for example one of conquest or of flight: 'In so far as a man's sexual history provides a key to his life, it is because in his sexuality is projected his manner of being towards the world, that is, towards time and other men.'[31]

So I *can* describe my relations with others, as I might do in therapy, but it is *this* that I am doing, describing an intricate web of connections, not describing some supposed and separate internal world. It is not, as Chris Oakley has written, that psychoanalytic accounts of psychic realities are irrelevant but that what they seek to describe should be seen in interpersonal rather than intrapsychic terms. A defence mechanism, for instance, is something that happens between people, in language, rather than 'in' one person or both.[32]

Adherence to a particular theory is not just a way of dealing with the therapeutic encounter, however. It is also a way of positioning oneself in the world of psychotherapy. 'What kind of therapist are you?' is, as I said in the introduction, a common question to anyone who declares himself a therapist. We need, it seems, to be able to place people, and to place ourselves, but too often this placing, whether of oneself or others, is limiting and restricting. So too can theory be used, not to communicate and engage in dialogue, but to intimidate and to establish a position of supposed superiority. But if we return to the origins of the word, we find not the notion of some definitive model, of supposed explanations set in stone, but rather something more tentative. The *theor* was someone sent by a community to visit a shrine or holy place and to report back on the experience, while *theoria* meant not only coherence of thought but voyage or spectacle, consulting the oracle, the place of the consultation, or speculation.

These meanings we have lost and while we might not be able to live without theories, we might try to be rather less dependent on them. It is possible, after all, to identify more than three hundred different schools of psychotherapy, each with its own theoretical base. Not only can not all be true but none has any greater proven clinical efficacy than the others. This, surely, should give us pause for thought. In its place we might think more in terms of *thoughtfulness*. This, as I shall argue later in this book, is what is called for from the psychotherapist, rather than adherence to a preconceived *system* into which everything has to be made to fit. As for clinical discussions we should think more in terms of what the anthropologist Clifford Geertz has termed 'thick description'. 'Why not say what happened?' as Robert Lowell proposed in one of his last poems, advising us to 'Pray for the grace of accuracy/ Vermeer gave to the sun's illumination/stealing like a tide across a map/to his girl solid with yearning'.[33]

We should recall too the inevitably autobiographical element in the theories of psychotherapy. The ideas of Freud, Klein, Jung and others, Jonathan Pedder has argued, owe a great deal to their own personal histories.[34] This does not, in itself, invalidate the theories; the experience of one person, whether it be Freud, Klein or whoever, is as valid as the experience of another, but it is no more so and attempts at generalising from relatively little evidence must be treated with scepticism.

THE RETREAT FROM THE SOCIAL

A detached observer of contemporary psychotherapy would be forced to conclude that this discipline is, in general, a conservative or apolitical one. She would get little or no idea of the radical political history of psychotherapy, the history of Ferenczi, Fenichel, Reich, Fromm, Lindner and many others. These are people who find little or no place on training courses, who have been consigned to the margins. Yet, whatever the personal views and commitments of Freud – and they were deeply ambiguous – these members of the second and third psychoanalytic generations, as Russell Jacoby has shown in his marvellous and moving book, *The Repression of Psychoanalysis: Otto Fenichel and the political Freudians*,[35] were steeped in the idea that their theory and practical work were inextricably connected to the world in which they were formed. Our observer would see a profession which, generally speaking, while politically liberal in political inclination, is profoundly conservative in its practice and position and which is, moreover, almost by definition cut off and isolated from the world outside the consulting room.

Now as soon as I say this, a number of important exceptions immediately spring to mind. Several hundred therapists and counsellors joined Psychotherapists and Counsellors for Social Responsibility when it was launched in 1995; the Free Associations project – the journal of the same name, the publishing imprint (at least in its original incarnation), the annual 'Psychoanalysis and the public sphere' conference and

41

so on – sought for nearly a decade to link the political and the social with the psychotherapeutic; and of course there is the profound and beneficial impact that the work of people associated with the Tavistock Clinic has had on health care and social work practice.

Yet, in general, therapists have kept apart from political or social involvement. Paradoxically this may not be a bad thing. I am sceptical about the value of political interventions which tell us, as some groups and writers have done, that war is 'all about' projective identification, or that political involvement is 'all about' reparation or 'doing therapy to the world'. Here too we fall into the trap of arrogance, of thinking we know, that we have 'the key' to understanding society (whatever that might mean). Here too we need a little humility. I shall return to this particular subject at greater length later in this book.

THE MYTH OF EVERYDAY UNHAPPINESS

Psychotherapy, at least in some of its forms, suffers too from a fundamental pessimism, a preoccupation with the negative, the dark side of human existence, what one might call the myth of ordinary unhappiness. There can be too much sense of life as endurance, as disappointment, and as struggle with the darker side of life. This is encapsulated by Freud's formulation about therapy merely changing 'neurotic misery' into 'everyday unhappiness', a remark that probably all therapists have trotted out at some point. But of course, as Cornelius Castoriadis stressed, ordinary unhappiness is not all that there is to life. (Freud, he suggested, came up with his phrase on 'one of his more discouraged days'.)[36]

This preoccupation with the negative seems to me to be part of the general mood of pessimism and negativism that followed the political failure of the protest movements of the

1960s and 1970s. It is surely no accident that it was in the wake of such defeats that so many intellectuals turned to thinkers who, in one way or another, tell us that there is no escape, no point in resistance or trying to change things, people who say, in effect, 'There is no point in trying to resist the oppressions and injustices of modern life, since even our dreams of freedom only add more links to our chains; however, once we grasp the total futility of it all, at least we can relax.'[37]

It is not that disappointment, unhappiness and tragedy do not exist. That they do and on a terrible scale cannot be denied and no psychotherapy worthy of the name can ignore them or play down their importance. But it is equally true that happiness and enjoyment exist. There are so many things in life that give us pleasure – our lovers, children, friends, books, music, films, places, drinking, eating and so on. These are not compensations for life and they are certainly not illusory. They are life, just as much as death, illness and suffering. Of course, what brings many people to seek therapy is precisely an inability or an attentuated ability to enjoy such things, in particular to make and sustain rewarding relationships. It is not a matter of pessimism or optimism, of whether one believes people are fundamentally bad or good, but of recognising that both good and bad exist and that human beings have a seemingly inexhaustible capacity for either, depending on their personal, social and historical circumstances. The Holocaust and the Gulag were the work of human beings just as much as such monumental creations as democracy or philosophy, as Castoriadis reminded us.[38] It is a matter of being able to hold the two together and recognise that the truth, as E. M. Forster puts it in *Howards End*, is not half-way between anything but is only to be found by 'continuous excursions into either realm'.

I can think of no better way of illustrating this than by quoting at length from a poem, 'Persuasion'. Its author,

Edwin Morgan, has written extensively throughout his life of
the darker aspects of human existence, the sadnesses, disap-
pointments, cruelties, poverty, violence; but he has also written of the other side of life, what he extolled in the work of
his fellow poet, Norman MacCaig, as 'the delights and
pleasures of steady perception of the possibility of ordinary
happiness'.[39] Morgan's own poem is a monologue in which
the poetic voice addresses another who has been the voice of
attempted persuasion to see the good things, who 'never
thought much of the darkness' and who 'wanted everything
so open . . .' and continues:

> Oh, never ask where darkness is if light can
> break down the very splinters of the jambs – be
> sure I know you can take in the sunlight
> through every pore and nothing will be blinded
> or shrivelled up like moth in flame or crippled
> by some excess of nakedness – just give it,
> your intelligence, your faith I really mean, your
> faith, that's it, to see the streets so brilliant
> after gales you really can go out there,
> you really can have something of that gladness,
> many things under the sun, and not disheartened,
> so many in their ways going beside you.[40]

Any gloss on this seems superfluous.

The task of the therapist is not persuasion as such but if
therapy is, as Bion said and as I believe, about helping people
to *dare* to be who they are, this must include the fostering of
a capacity for enjoyment or pleasure. This capacity is something that is there in almost everyone who seeks therapy and
will be clear in the things that people do take pleasure in,
often from impersonal activities such as eating, drinking,
listening to music, looking at paintings and so on, however
limited this might be. And as I have suggested, the very fact

44

that a person seeks therapy suggests a desire for greater aliveness in this sense. But this is always a struggle which is why, I think, so many people find it difficult in therapy to admit to pleasure or enjoyment. To this end there comes a time, perhaps in every therapy, when it is part of the task of the therapist to put into question, to disrupt, the stories that people tell themselves and others about themselves, especially when these stories are inhibiting and constraining and when they are only a *part* of the truth.

CONCLUSION

These, it seems to me, are some of the faults of psychotherapy and psychotherapists; they constitute much of what is wrong with psychotherapy today. The project of psychotherapy is not vitiated by them however, although it is compromised. Psychotherapy, then, has to find ways of renewing itself, of engaging once again in a self-critical, self-reflective stance. The philosopher Merleau-Ponty wrote nearly thirty years ago that psychoanalysis needed philosophy, and in particular his own variant of philosophical thought, phenomenology, in order *to be what it is*. So it is my belief that psychotherapy needs a new encounter, not with science, not with the white coat of the laboratory, but with philosophy, with ideas about ideas, thought about thinking, particularly about what happens in a room when two individual human subjects meet – or at least try to. In particular, I believe, psychotherapy has a great deal to gain from an encounter with a number of thinkers not normally admitted to the world of psychotherapeutic thought, people like Mikhail Bakhtin, Gaston Bachelard and (in this country at least) Cornelius Castoriadis, as well as a number of poets. Above all, I believe, psychotherapy has much to learn from the uncompromising ethical thought of Emmanuel Levinas, in order to be what it is. And it is to this that I now turn.

2

'Vigilant passivity to the call of the other': therapy as ethics

The essential problem is: can we speak of an absolute commandment after Auschwitz? Can we speak of morality after the failure of morality?

Emmanuel Levinas[1]

In the context of the simplicity that I mentioned in the introduction, it might seem bizarre, perverse even, to speak of the extraordinarily rich and complex work of the French and Jewish philospher Emmanuel Levinas, thought which, as Derrida has so beautifully put it, can make us tremble. But it is Levinas, more than any other thinker of our times, who again and again returns – and returns us – to the simple things, the everyday things: what it is to feel fatigued, to suffer insomnia, to caress a loved one, to savour food, to shake the hand of a friend, above all what it is to encounter another human subject.

What *does* it mean to encounter another human being? What is the meaning of my responsibility to that other? No psychotherapist can avoid these questions which are at the heart of the psychotherapeutic endeavour. No one has posed these questions more radically, more intransigently, and suggested answers more than Emmanuel Levinas. More than any other philosopher this century, Levinas, who was born in 1906 and died in 1995, placed ethics at the heart of philos-

46

ophy. In a series of books, including *Existence and Existents* (started during the privations of a German forced labour camp), *Time and the Other*, the dense, almost other-worldly prose of *Totality and Infinity* and *Otherwise than Being or Beyond Essence*, as well as in many articles and interviews, Levinas proposed an understanding of our being in the world and, above all else, our way of being *with others* that is radically at odds with established thought.* In particular, Levinas argued that ethics is responsibility for the other, that this responsibility precedes knowledge and, moreover, has nothing whatsoever to do with reciprocity, that is I do not do something in order to get something in return. Furthermore, Levinas argued, it is this ethical responsibility which *constitutes me as a subject*, it *is* the meaning of my subjectivity.

Ethics, in the very particular sense that Levinas gives it, is at the heart of psychotherapy, but ethics in this sense requires that we abandon a great many preconceptions and assumptions about otherness and about our relations with others, that we have to develop an attitude or position of radical openness towards the other in all his strangeness which avoids reducing the other to what is already known to us.

Levinas's work can be seen as a sustained contestation of the preoccupation in Western thought with knowledge in which even other human subjects are treated as phenomena to be known and to be understood, as a result of which they are appropriated and reduced to the same as the supposed

---

* Reference to Levinas's work in this chapter is made as follows: *EE* – *Existence and Existents* (trans. A. Lingis), Kluwer Academic Publishers, Dordrecht, 1978; *EI* – *Ethics and Infinity: conversations with Philippe Nemo* (trans. R. A. Cohen), Duquesne University Press, Pittsburgh, 1985; 'EP' – 'Ethics as first philosophy' in *The Levinas Reader*, S. Hand (ed.), Blackwell, Oxford, 1989; *NTR* – *Nine Talmudic Readings* (trans. A. Aronowicz), Indiana University Press, Bloomington, 1990; *TI* – *Totality and Infinity: an essay on exteriority* (trans. A. Lingis), Duquesne University Press, Pittsburgh, 1969; *TO* – *Time and the Other* (trans. R. A. Cohen), Duquesne University Press, Pittsburgh, 1987.

knower. In this process their essential and fundamental otherness is lost. At one point Levinas caustically remarks that philosophy can be defined as 'the subordination of any act to the knowledge that one may have of that act, knowledge being precisely this merciless demand to bypass nothing' (*NTR*, p.35). One might say the same of much psychotherapeutic theorising which allows nothing to escape its grasp. Beyond such knowledge, Levinas suggests, there is a 'more urgent form [of being] . . . that of wisdom' (*EP*, p.78).

Levinas's work is a radical departure from the dominant philosophical modes of thinking about ethics and ethical responsibility. Above all, it emphasises the *asymmetry* of the ethical relationship. It insists that the ethical responsibility towards the other exists *prior* to the relationship. Not only is Levinas's position quite opposed to that of someone like Sartre for whom the other is an intrusion and threat ('Hell is other people' to quote the famous – and preposterous – line from *Huis Clos*) but it is something quite other too from seemingly more benign and equal views of the other. The 'I-Thou' relationship of Martin Buber, for instance, is essentially symmetrical since it implies that I expect to be treated by the other as Thou also. Not only that, but the relationship is a means to an end in that it is the guarantee of my own being. So too Levinas's ethics means something quite different to Heidegger's idea of *Mitsein* or being-with for this too implies symmetry and is in any case essentially, as Levinas commented, content-less: 'being-with-another is but a moment of our presence in the world. It does not occupy central place. *Mit* means to be aside of . . . it is not to confront the Face . . .',[2] *Mitsein* or being-with goes far, to be sure, but Levinas argues that one must go further, that it is not enough to be with, one must meet the other face to face as it were.

The Levinasian notion of ethics goes against the grain of thought which sees in the other only a version of my self,

which appropriates the other through some assumed knowledge or claimed understanding. The problem of postmodern
paralysis – a situation in which, for some, we can know
nothing, where there are no secure foundations, and, in a
sense, anything goes in a world where no meaningful value
judgements or distinctions can be made – is not that everything is permitted, and by means of technology, possible, but
that:

> [E]verything has become indifferent. The unknown is
> immediately rendered familiar and the new habitual. There
> is nothing new under the sun. The crisis spoken of in
> Ecclesiastes is not due to sin but to ennui. Everything
> becomes absorbed, engulfed and immured in the Same . . .
> Everywhere one suspects and denounces the machinations
> of spectacle, the transcendence of empty rhetoric, play.
> Vanity of vanities, the echo of our own voices, taken as a
> response to what few entreaties remain to us, everywhere
> fallen back onto our own feet, as after the ecstasies of a
> drug. Except the other who, in all this ennui, one cannot
> abandon.[3]

Against this Levinas argues that 'there is no exceptional
place for the subject' (*TO*, p.83). ' "To be or not to be?" – is
that the question?' asks Levinas. 'Is it the first and final
question?' Does being human mean forcing oneself to be?
No, Levinas answers; the question of the meaning of being is
not the ontology of that 'extraordinary verb' but the ethics of
its justice. 'The question par excellence or the question of
philosophy. Not "Why being rather than nothing?" but how
being justifies itself' (*EP*, p.86).

The other is not only an alter ago; 'the Other is what I
myself am not'. The other is this, not because of his character,
or physiognomy or psychology, but because of his very

alterity. 'The Other is, for example, the weak, the poor,"the widow and the orphan", whereas I am the rich and powerful . . . intersubjective space is not symmetrical' (*TO* pp. 83–4).

RESPONSIBILITY FOR THE OTHER

The nature of the relationship with the other is fundamentally that of *responsibility for* the other; as Levinas beautifully states it: 'The tie with the Other is knotted only as responsibility. To say "Here I am".'⁴ As one of Levinas's interlocutors remarks, responsibility means being for (not merely being-aside or even being-with) the other. And this being-for is unconditional (that is, if it is to be moral, not merely contractual) – it does not depend on what the other is, or does, whether he deserves my care and whether he repays in kind.⁵

Responsibility as responsibility for the other means in Levinas's terms that I am responsible for what is not my deed, or for what does not even matter to me. In other words, it does not matter what the other has done or may have done.

The other 'does not appear as belonging to an order which can be "embraced" or "grasped". The other in this relationship of responsibility is, as it were, unique: "unique" meaning without genre. In this sense he is absolutely other, not only in relation to me; he is alone as if he were the only one of significance at that moment.'⁶ This other is the only thing that matters to me at this moment.

To reiterate, the intersubjective relation, the relationship of responsibility, is emphatically a non-symmetrical relation.'In this sense, I am responsible for the Other without waiting for reciprocity, were I to die for it. Reciprocity is *his* affair.' Indeed, for Levinas it is precisely because the relationship is not symmetrical or reciprocal that I am subjection to the other. Levinas often quoted this sentence of Dostoevsky from *The Brothers Karamazov*: 'We are all guilty of all and for all men before all, and I more than the others.' What this means according to Levinas is that I am responsible for a total responsibility which answers for all the others and for all in the others, even for their responsibility: 'The I always has one responsibility *more* than all the others' (*EI*, pp. 98–9).

This non-reciprocity or asymmetry is emphasised by Bauman:

> I am for the Other whether the Other is for me or not; his being for me is, so to speak, his problem, and whether or not he 'handles' that problem does not in the least affect my being-for-him (as far as my being-for-the Other includes respect for the Other's autonomy, which in its turn includes my consent not to blackmail the Other into being-for-me, nor interfere in any other way in the Other's freedom). Whatever else 'I-for-you' may contain, it does not contain a demand to be repaid, mirrored or 'balanced out' in the 'you-for-me'. My relation to the Other is not reversible; if it happens to be reciprocated, the reciprocation is but an accident from the point of view of my being-for.[7]

Nor does my responsibilty have anything to do with the proximity of the other, whether in space, because for instance he is a neighbour, or by virtue of some particular relationship, for instance because we belong to the same family; nor does it have anything to do with knowledge. 'The tie with the Other is knotted only as responsibility' (*EI*, p. 97) and this holds, moreover, whether the responsibility is accepted or refused, whether I know or know not how to assume it, whether I am able or unable to do something concrete for the other.

This responsibility, moreover, is the essential, primary and fundamental structure of subjectivity. It is what constitutes me as a human subject. Ethics does not supplement a preceding existential base; it is not something added on to my being;

rather 'the very node of the subjective is knotted in ethics understood as responsibility' (*EI*, p. 95). Responsibility is not an attribute of subjectivity, as if subjectivity already existed in itself, before the ethical relationship: 'Subjectivity is not for itself; it is once again, initially for another' (*EI,* p. 96). Responsibility for the other, Levinas says elsewhere, 'establishes the ego. To be a self is to be responsible beyond what one has oneself done' (*NTR*, p. 49). I exist through the other, Levinas says elsewhere, and for the other but this is not alienation as in other schemas: 'The word *I* means *here I am* answering for everything and everyone.'[8]

Levinas's notion of responsibilty is not without its problems. How can one really be responsibile in the way he suggests? Am I really responsible for what is done by others? Can one really disregard the seemingly human tendency to feel more for those with whom we have a more proximate relationship, our family, friends and neighbours? There is something overwhelming about the demands imposed by Levinas's ethics. We are, moreover, being asked to enter such an ethical relationship not on the basis of logical argument – this would be anathema to Levinas – but on trust, or as a matter of faith, coming as it does as a pre-ordained fact, from 'beyond being'.

The point however is not to answer these questions but rather to enter into a dialogue, into a conversation with Levinas. At the very least he calls into question our narrow assumptions and preconceptions and shakes us, if we allow it, out of our assumptions and complacencies.

As far as the practice of psychotherapy is concerned, Levinas's understanding of responsibility seems to me directly relevant to what we do. Here we are concerned solely with this person before us. What he has done or may have done is, in a sense, not our business. We are not here to judge, to grant forgiveness or condemn. And of course the psychotherapeutic relationship is not a reciprocal one. As a psychotherapist, I am there for this other: he is not there for me. Finally, the psychotherapist is not distant. He is in there. In a sense he is the other, prepared to abandon his own ego, to take the place of the other. This does not mean a taking over but a standing in the place of, a substitution for. 'I do not ask the wounded person how he feels ... I myself become the wounded person,' as Walt Whitman puts it in his *Song of Myself*. The ethical relationship puts the I in question, in the practice of psychotherapy as elsewhere. In psychotherapy, as Steve Gans has said, the suffering of the other exposes us to the fundamental dimension of ethics, to the face of the other, and to the basic ethical dilemma, how do we respond to the other's pain and suffering. As Levinas puts it:

> Is not the evil of suffering – extreme passivity, impotence, abandonment and solitude – also the unassimilable and thus the possibility of a half-opening, and more precisely, the possibiity that wherever a moan, a cry, a groan or a sigh has passed there is the original call for aid, for curative help, for help from the other ego whose alterity, whose exteriority promises solution?[9]

THE FACE

The notion of ethical responsibilty is inextricably tied to what Levinas calls 'the face'. Levinas, it has to be acknowledged, is not consistent in his use of this idea; he uses it variously to mean the very identity of a being, personal expression that does not need to be cognitively perceived by others, or the way in which the other presents himself, that is a summons or call to be obeyed. Whatever, the face is certainly not to be understood literally, nor even metaphorically, but rather poetically, although Levinas has certainly observed the power of the literal face to face relationship. It is harder to kill someone whose face one looks into; the face of the person to be executed is masked or their head hooded; people are shot in the back of the head. It is from this that the notion derives. For Levinas it is the face that gives access to the ethical demand; the face *is* a demand. 'The face is a hand in search of recompense, an open hand. That is, it needs something. It is going to ask you for something.' One's reaction to the face is a response but also a responsibility.[10]

The approach to the face is the most basic mode of responsibility. The face of the other is not in front of me but above me, 'it spells a relation of rectitude' and asserts the primacy of the other. Not only does the face say to me, 'You shall not kill,' it exposes me 'as a usurper of the place of the other'. My supposed 'right to existence' is challenged by the relation to the face and my duty to respond to the other suspends my right to self-survival:

> To expose myself to the vulnerability of the face is to put my ontological right to existence into question. In ethics, the other's right to exist has primacy over my own, a primacy epitomized in the ethical edict: you shall not kill, you shall not jeopardize the life of the other. The ethical rapport with the face is asymmetrical in that it subordinates my existence to the other.[11]

For Levinas the face is always given as countenance: 'We meet this countenance in the look of the other, and it doesn't declare itself: but behind it there is the weakness.' The face is an epiphany, something that shows without mediation: 'The epiphany of the other person is *ipso facto* my responsibility toward him: seeing the other is already an obligation toward him. A direct optics – without the mediation of any idea – can only be accomplished as ethics' (*NTR*, p. 47). The face cannot be contained, comprehended or encompassed: 'the face speaks to me and thereby invites me to a relation incommensurate with a power exercised, be it enjoyment or knowledge' (*TI*, p. 198). (Comprehension, as Levinas says in an interview, is part of the problem that he is addressing, in that it involves taking, appropriating, 'always the fact of making something one's own'. But there is always something that remains outside and that is alterity which is unencompassable.[12])

The face cannot be reduced to what is available to perception. Levinas writes that 'access to the face is straightaway ethical. You turn yourself toward the other as toward an object when you can see a nose, eyes, a forehead, a chin, and you can describe them. The best way of encountering the Other is not even to notice the colour of his eyes! When one observes the color of the eyes one is not in social relationship with the Other' (*EI*, p. 85).

One can, of course, choose to ignore the demand of the face; the commandment, 'You shall not kill' is breached all the time. The face, as Levinas remarks, is not a force but an authority and authority is often without force.[13] This relation, 'the look meeting look, the face facing a face', is a relation 'shot through with a moment of commitment'. But this commitment is unlike all others: 'it is not a product of the subject's intentionality; it is not wanted, it simply imposes itself as a property pertaining to the very structure of this dyad of proximity'.[14]

Again in relation to the face what is affirmed is the asymmetry of the ethical relationship; 'in the beginning it does not matter to me who the Other is, that is his business.' Bauman remarks that this can be read as a definition of the face:

Face is encountered if, and only if, my relation to the Other is *programmatically* non-symmetrical, that is, not dependent on the Other's past, present, anticipated or hoped-for reciprocation. And morality is the encounter with the Other as Face. Moral stance begets an essentially unequal

55

relationship; this inequality, non-equity, this not-asking-for reciprocation, this disinterest in mutuality, this indifference to the 'balancing up' of gains and rewards – in short, this organically 'unbalanced' and hence non-reversible charac-ter of 'I versus the Other' relationship is what makes the encounter a moral event.[15]

The face, as Jonathan Rée remarks, is really two-faced, facing two ways:

It is at once what faces us and what we face. And if we take care never to forget this ambiguity, we may save ourselves from the worst but easiest of crimes: the violence that forgets that others are the subjects of their own experiences, that they will always have their own unex-pected stories to tell. We will remember that, however well we understand someone else, there will always be some-thing left over, that they face their experience, but we face only them.[16]

The face is a command: 'do not leave me in solitude . . . here is my responsibility for the other'.[17] 'Do not leave me in solitude' – is this not what those who seek psychotherapy are saying? The notion of the face to face makes us pause to think about the classical psychoanalytic setting with the patient on the couch, his face hidden, unseen. Yes, lying down may well facilitate free association but how much is missed! The patient who sits on the chair facing me rather than lying down on the couch wishes not just to see but to be seen. It is on or rather in the other's face that I may see so many things – a smile, sadness, fear, anxiety, despair, boredom – before this is articulated in words. So too can the couch be a hiding place for the psychotherapist, just as it was for Freud who advocated its use, in part, because he hated being looked at all day. With the patient on the couch, the therapist can hide his feelings, fatigue, boredom, irritation, distraction. It can, in short, be a way of hiding himself. But the face is not just or even primarily a source of emotional information, but a continuous call, a constant command, and it is this which, quite understandably, we find draining and exhausting and from which we seek refuge.

THE CONTENT OF RESPONSIBILITY

We cannot know in advance what the content of our responsibility towards the other will be, what it will require of us, what demands it will place upon us. Nor can we know beforehand *how* we should respond, what we shall have to do. There are no rules or codes to guide us. To use a word much loved by Levinas, we are *hostage* to the other. Responsibility, Bauman writes, comes 'both empty, waiting to be filled, and infinite, unlikely ever to be ful-filled.'[18] In this context, rules and codes are, as the ethical philosopher Logs-trup says, 'a means of keeping aloof from one another and for insulating ourselves.'[19] So too Levinas himself remarks caustically how the 'Marvellous alterity of the Other has been banalized and dimmed in an exchange of courtesies which became established as an "interpersonal commerce" of customs.'[20] Bauman adds that the 'rule-governed togetherness, the being-with exhausted in the observance of rules' is but 'a colony of hermits, an archipelago of one-resident islands'. It also allows for an interaction that is devoid of sentiment save those which are focused on the *'procedure* of interaction'.[21]

The participatory empathic attitude, Bauman emphasises, is always and irreparably a personal stance, personally taken – 'it is endemically erratic, shuns codification, cannot be taught or obtained by rote learning'. For this very reason, 'the world of ethics, the world of regularity, codes, teaching and learning has no room for empathy and emotional participation in the sufferings of the Other.'[22]

Nor is taking up responsibility itself enough. It is rather 'a necessary but woefully insufficient condition of goodness. The exercise of responsibility means steering for ever a course between good and evil without the succour of certainty or authoritative reassurance, without hope of ever drawing the last, definite and uncontestable line between the two.'[23]

A lot of confusion arises in discussions about Levinas's work from ascribing a single meaning to the notion of 'responsibility'. Often, it seems, responsibility is taken to mean the same as caring, as in the Biblical example, which admittedly Levinas was fond of, of the good Samaritan who does physically attend to the stranger he finds by the wayside. But this is certainly not the only meaning of responsibility. I am responsible *for* my children (among others) and have a responsibilty *to* them, but this does not mean giving them what they want. Indeed, part of my responsibility is in teaching them that they cannot have everything they want. My responsibility to and for them involves the setting of limitations as much as anything else. Of course I will do this in a way that involves them in dialogue appropriate to their ages, but ultimately I may have to impose my decision. Similarly, I have no doubt that I have a responsibility to people sleeping or begging in the streets. But my responsibility may most effectively be exercised by some form of political or social action as opposed to offering them a bed for the night. This does not preclude giving some money directly to the person but this is far from being the end of the matter. In a more extreme case, my responsibility to the other may require what may seem at first sight hostile to that other. To take an example whose spirit is everywhere present in Levinas's work, what would be my responsibility to the torturer, the mass murderer? Would not my responsibility entail seeking justice and appropriate punishment? To be sure I can try to understand such a person – as Gitta Sereny does in her inquiry into the thinking and motivations of Hitler's architect and armaments minister, Albert Speer, an ethical study without parallel[24] – but responsibility to them and to others requires something else. Responsibility, in other words, has many, many meanings.

'Without the succour of certainty or authoritative reassurance' – this could be, should be a motto for the psychotherapist. Contrary to common belief there are no rules, no techniques. 'Ethical codes' to which we are required to adhere if we wish to be registered surely only tell us what we already know. It is not that 'anything goes' but that what goes is a matter each of us has to work out for ourselves.

ETHICS AND LANGUAGE, THE SAYING AND THE SAID

The notion of responsibility is for Levinas inextricably tied to language. Indeed, Levinas goes so far as to say that 'the beginning of language is in the face. In a certain way, in its silence, it calls you.' My reaction to this call is not just a response but a responsibility. (The two words are, of course, closely related.) Language does not begin with the signs that one gives, with words. Rather, 'Language is above all the fact of being addressed . . .'[25] Elsewhere Levinas says that speech in its original essence is 'a commitment to a third party on behalf of our neighbour; the act *par excellence*, the institution of society. The original function of speech consists not in designating an object in order to communicate with the other in a game with no consequences but in assuming toward someone a responsibility on behalf of someone else. To speak is to engage the interests of men. Responsibility would be the essence of language' (*NTR*, p. 21).

In his later work, notably *Otherwise than Being or Beyond*

Essence, Levinas makes a distinction between what he calls the *saying* and the *said*. The former, which Levinas describes as 'ethical sincerity', is irreducible to the latter. 'Saying is what makes the self-exposure of sincerity possible; it is a way of giving everything, of not keeping anything for oneself . . . Language as saying is an ethical openness to the other.' That which is said, on the other hand, is reduced to a fixed identity and amounts to closure to the other. The child who has not yet learned to dissemble, to deceive, to be insincere, is a pure exposure or expression in so far as he is pure vulnerability.[26]

The saying is my response to the other, whether verbal or not, the content of which cannot be captured in rules or propositions: 'The Saying is the sheer radicality of human speaking, of the event of being in relation with an Other; it is the non-thematizable ethical residue of language that escapes comprehension, interrupts philosophy and is the very enactment of the ethical movement from the same to the Other.'[27] By contrast the said is a statement, a proposition or assertion.

The two orders of discourse, furthermore, do not occur in the same time. The said exists in synchrony, a bringing together in a unified order of time; the saying exists in diachrony, a coming apart of time, dispersed time.

We can see this distinction at work in the practice of psychotherapy, in that gap between what actually happens in a session and any attempt to record or reconstruct it afterwards. No matter how good one's memory appears to be, no matter how much one seems to be able to recall of the patient's speech as well as one's own, something, and something important I believe, is invariably lost. Indeed, the two events – the session and the session as it has been reconstructed – can seem curiously unrelated. Yes, the same two people are present and the words recorded may be a good enough recollection or approximation of what was said, but what is lost – what cannot be recaptured – is all the manner of the saying, the ebb and flow of the conversation, its textures and tones, above all perhaps the sense of openness, of contingency, of indeterminacy. This is why even recordings do not work. The recording, whether audio or video, freezes something that was once alive, puts bounds around something that was free or striving to be so. Levinas himself has observed how even poetry which has the power to transform words and disrupt order can yet, by virtue of its cultural and social context, be tamed and become 'engulfed in order . . . solidify into a narrative, still envelop itself in the totality of the *said*'.[28] (An example of this would be the fate of Paul Celan's great poem 'Todesfuge' which seemed in danger of losing its disruptive or unsettling power as it gave post-war Germans relief for their guilt, to the point that the poet refused to allow the poem to be anthologised or used in readings.)

What Levinas has to say about the distinction between the saying and the said is important and salutary. However, an obvious problem exists, and it is one 'that haunts every page of *Otherwise than Being*'[29] – how the saying can be given expression. The fact that something is said does not necessarily lead to closure, to fixity. The simplest statement, as much as the most complex, is made to someone else and can be the opening up of a dialogue or conversation. Even a statement of incontrovertible and simple fact – 'The cat is on the mat' – is not necessarily the end of the matter but may be the beginning. 'What is the cat doing?' I might ask. 'Is it a live cat or a dead one?', 'How do you know?', 'Is that really important?' and so on. Nevertheless it is all too easy to see how the said does become fixed and closed, an end of dialogue. In the field of psychotherapy, for instance, what is said – in the form of papers and books – can all too easily solidify into dogma, something to be defended by its adherents rather than engaged with in a living way.

But the problem here is not just about the difference between a psychotherapy session and its recording or recollection, however this is done. Levinas's distinction between the saying and the said is a warning to us against a tendency to seek closure, to impose order. It is part of our responsibility to the other to allow for openness, formlessness, dis-order. Psychotherapists are, I suggest, notoriously bad at this. We have our theories and what we see is supposed to fit into these. The psychotherapist well versed in a particular theory, John Heaton remarks, finds that theory wherever he looks: 'The Freudian finds Oedipal themes, the Kleinian the presence or absence of the depressive position, the Jungian various stages of individuation, and so on. Psychotherapy, wherever it looks, only finds itself; a form of violence to the Other', violence in the sense that it is not truly open to the other and his story but comes to the encounter with a preconceived schema.[30] So too Steve Gans remarks, 'To allow the Other to be means to let someone speak independently, apart from any other aim we have in regard to that person. We cannot place the Other in our own light, and incorporate the Other into our own story, without destroying the possibility of meeting in the genuine sense.'[31] Putting the other first, Gans says, 'can only take place in saying, in the intimacy of relatedness, rather than in the domain of the abstract and impersonal everything said'.[32] What such a genuine meeting might involve is something to which the rest of this book is devoted.

3

Language, listening and dialogue: the therapeutic conversation

To say more than human things with human voice,
That cannot be; to say human things with more
Than human voice, that, also cannot be;
To speak humanly from the height or from the depth
Of human things, that is acutest speech.

Wallace Stevens[1]

The ethical stance that is the practice of psychotherapy calls for a particular kind of listening and engagement, a particular kind of conversation and dialogue. Psychotherapy is frequently referred to as the 'talking cure' but this is misleading. Talking – or indeed not talking – is only one side or aspect of the process of psychotherapy; what of 'the other side of language', what of listening, what of language itself? These are matters to which therapists give too little thought. Like so much else we take language for granted. How little it is discussed or thought about. Indeed, it is possible to train as a psychotherapist without ever discussing the meaning of language, yet language is central to what we do. If there were no language (an impossibility of course) there could be no therapy. Imagine a world where architects were not required to understand building materials, doctors to understand human physiology or cooks to understand food. The idea is absurd. As for listening, if it

63

is discussed at all – and it rarely is – it is reduced to some kind of technique.

Psychotherapists take language too much for granted. We think little, too little, about it, as though it presents no problems, and this taking for granted leads us too often into a false way of thinking about what language means, about what it means to speak. Too often we think facilely of language as a 'means of communication' or of something we need to express our thoughts, what is in our minds.

The idea that speech somehow translates thought that is ready-made, 'in the mind', is a nonsense. Speech, as Merleau-Ponty showed, does not translate thought so much as *accomplish* it.[2] Language is not a translation of thought; conversely thought is not an ideal text that our sentences translate. The author has no text with which he can compare his writing, and no language prior to language. 'His speech satisfies him only because it reaches an equilibrium whose conditions his speech itself defines, and attains a state of perfection which has no model.' Language does not presuppose a table of correspondence, 'it unveils its secrets itself, it teaches them to every child who comes into the world. It is entirely a "monstration".'[3]

So too Wittgenstein remarks that saying something like 'to express an idea that is before our mind' suggests that what we are trying to express in words is already expressed, only in a different language; that this expression is before our mind's eye; and that what we do is to translate from the mental into the verbal language. Wittgenstein rejects this. It is the very expression or usage that constitutes social reality.[4]

If we rid ourselves of the idea that language is the translation or cipher of an original text, then we see that the idea of 'complete expression' is a nonsense and that all language is indirect or allusive.[5] This is important for psychotherapists who so often are faced with people who have profound difficulties expressing themselves and who may be able to utter only fragments of speech. Our task is not to wait until such fragments become more whole but rather to attend to these shards and their meaning at this moment for this person.

What then does language express, if it does not express thoughts? 'It presents or rather it *is* the subject's taking up of a position in the world of his meanings', Merleau-Ponty says.[6] Language is what makes us human. 'Whoever says man says language,' Levi-Strauss wrote, 'and whoever says language says society.'[7] One of our most common words shows this. The very word person, George Steiner reminds us, derives from the Latin *personare*, literally to sound through.[8]

Language, in other words, is constitutive of human beings, of who we are. 'I become a person and remain one only as an interlocutor,' Charles Taylor concludes from his discussion of what it is to be a person. It creates what Taylor calls 'a public space', a common vantage point from which we survey the world together. A crucial feature of language for Taylor is that 'it creates the peculiarly human kind of rapport, of being together, that we are in conversation together. To express something, to formulate it can be not only to get in articulate focus, but also to place it in public space, and thus to bring us together qua participants in a common act of focussing.'

Language brings things into 'articulate focus' and into public space. Even our solitary conversations, our conversations with ourselves, depend on the language that we could only learn in conversation, while our public conversations, public that is even with one other person, are essential to formulating things:

Thus our grasp on our emotions, on what is deep and what is superficial, what is fundamental commitment, and what is passing fancy, what is profound love and what is mere dalliance, can depend crucially on our conversations with others. By which I mean that we can often doubt our own grasp of these terms, that is, our own discriminations made with them, where we can come to an understanding with others on these discriminations. This is not just a matter of using other people as checks on ourselves, tests of our understanding; it is also that we can need other people, the conversation and understanding with them, even to come clear on what it is we feel. The matter can come to clear formulation when the agency focussing is *us* (for some favoured interlocutor or group) and not simply *me*.[9]

Language, to cite Merleau-Ponty again, is 'much more like a sort of being than a means, and this is why it can present something to us so well. A friend's speech over the telephone brings us the friend himself, as if he were wholly present in that manner of calling and saying goodbye to us, of beginning and ending his sentences, and of carrying on the conversation through things left unsaid. *Because meaning is the total movement of speech our thought crawls along in language.*'[10] Elsewhere, Merleau-Ponty quotes Goldstein:

As soon as man uses language to establish a living relation with himself or with his fellows, language is no longer an instrument, no longer a means; it is a manifestation, a revelation of intimate being and of the psychic link which unites us to the world and our fellow men.[11]

It is sometimes said, following Heidegger, that man does not speak language but that language speaks man or through him, 'language remains the master of man' as Heidegger puts it.[12] This is certainly true sometimes. Writing or speaking, I may surprise myself as it were, putting words on the page or saying something that I had not planned to say and, if I am fortunate, I may feel that I have put something particularly well, come up with a striking image, a particularly arresting formulation. Many who have written of the creative process (and not just in writing) speak precisely of a letting go, of allowing the words (or action) to come *through one*, as it were. And yet at the same time, at this moment I am choosing to write *these* words – about language – and not others – about the weather or cooking – in the same way that those who say 'language speaks us' are choosing to say *these* words and not 'the sun has got its hat on' or 'all psychotherapists look grey in the park'.

While it is true that I do not 'own' meaning, as some theorists would have it, it is also not true that no one owns it. Rather *we*, that is the human collectivity, own meaning or, at least, we can rent it or share in it, with one voice taking its place with that of others, one, few or many.

THE DIALOGICAL PRINCIPLE

No one has better understood the centrality of language in the construction of the social world and in the nature of human beings and human communication than the Russian thinker Mikhail Bakhtin, who coined the term dialogism. For Bakhtin, there is no knowledge of the human subject that is not formed through words, through language, that is not dialogical, since the human subject cannot be studied as though it were a thing, since it cannot remain a subject if it is voiceless. Indeed, life itself is by its very nature dialogical since to live means 'to engage in dialogue, to question, to listen, to answer, to agree, etc.'[13]

For Bakhtin, *all* verbal interaction takes place in the form of an exchange of utterances, that is the form of the dialogue.[14] The 'utterance' is inescapably social:

No utterance in general can be attributed to the speaker exclusively; it is the product of the interaction of the interlocutors, and, broadly speaking, the product of the whole complex social situation in which it has occurred.[15]

Language, in other words, is not mine. It belongs to, comes from and returns to the human community of which I am a part and in which I participate through language. This has profound implications for what it means to be a person. The dialogical principle insists that we are immediately and irretrievably social. This runs counter to much of Western thought with its belief in the idea of a sovereign individual. Most psychology is part of this way of thinking. So too is most of the theory underlying the various forms of psychotherapy.

The word, Bakhtin maintains again and again, is fundamentally social, not private:

The word does not exist in a neutral and impersonal language (it is not, after all, out of a dictionary that the speaker gets his word), but rather it exists in other people's mouths, in other people's contexts, serving other people's intentions; it is from there that one must take the word and make it one's own ... Language is not a neutral medium that passes freely and easily into the private property of the speaker's intentions; it is populated – overpopulated – with the intentions of others.[16]

Not a single instance of verbal utterance can be reckoned exclusively to its utterer's account. Every utterance is *the product of the interaction of the speakers*, and the product of the broader context of the whole complex *social situation* in which the utterance emerges.[17]

In point of fact, *word is a two-sided act*. It is determined equally by *whose* word it is and *for whom* it is meant. As word, it is precisely *the product of the reciprocal relationship between speaker and listener, addresser and addressee* . . . A word is a bridge thrown between myself and another. If one end of the bridge depends on me, then the other depends on my addressee. A word is territory shared by both addressee, by the speaker and the interlocutor.[18]

Todorov compares this to Levinas: 'Expression, before being a celebration of being, is a *relation* to whoever it is to whom I express the expression and whose presence is already required for my cultural gesture of expression to be produced.'[19]

This way of understanding speech and language has profound implications for the practice of psychotherapy. Psychologists and psychotherapists have been to a marked degree monologic, asserting the primacy of the individual, failing even to see that the very idea of the individual is a social concept. Theories underlying psychotherapy again and again assert the primacy of the one over the other, a fear of the other even who is seen as hostile and intrusive. Otherness, it seems, is always threatening, a source of danger. Even in interpersonal theories, apparently more acknowledging of the importance of the other, this other is experienced only as an adjunct to the self, inevitably secondary and supplementary.

Our entry into and acquisition of language is invariably social as well as intellectual, but it is also emotional. In his book *Seeing Voices*, Oliver Sacks tells the story of two deaf Italian boys. One, Joseph, had 'an anguished sense of something missing', unable to communicate even simple thoughts by Sign. Another, Manuel, lacked language of any kind but was bright, affectionate and emotionally normal and, once he entered a school for the deaf, quickly acquired both Sign and Italian. For Sacks the difference lay in the fact that Manuel, although regarded as different by his family, was never seen as alien, was always loved and always involved. By contrast, Joseph was regarded as autistic or retarded and suffered an 'annihilating sense of left-outness and isolation'.[20] Manuel was, in other words, included in his family's emotional world while Joseph was not.

In his searching critique of Freudianism from a dialogical perspective, Bakhtin remarked that Freud had taken for individual attributes what was truly social. What is reflected in the verbal utterances of the patient in psychoanalysis, for example, is not the dynamics of the individual psyche, as Freud claimed, but 'the social dynamics of the interrelations of doctor and patient'.[21] Freud's system projects the entire dynamics of the interrelationship between two people into the individual psyche.[22]

Bakhtin posed a questioning reversal of the psychoanalytic session:

> Would it not be more correct to say that the physician and the patient, having joined forces, are doing nothing but projecting into the unconscious complex (paternal or maternal) their present relations, inherent to the treatment (more precisely, some aspects of them, or their general schema, since these relations are very complex):[23]

The dialogical principle teaches us a number of things:

> First of all, we are fundamentally and irretrievably dialogic, conversational creatures whose lives are created in and through conversations and sustained or transformed in and through conversations. We learn that the very processes of our mind – including how we think, how we reason, how we know, how we solve problems, and so forth – are best grasped by examining the conversations in the social worlds we inhabit, which we appropriate and use. We learn that the qualities of our personality and identity are likewise

constituted conversationally and sustained through our dialogues with various others.[24]

It reminds us that the process by which our selves are constituted is never finished, that dialogues are not something that we can simply enter and leave, that life is dialogic.[25]

THE ART OF LISTENING

> *Not knowing how to listen, neither can they speak.*
>
> Heraclitus

> *Attentiveness is the natural prayer of the soul.*
>
> Malebranche

The 'talking cure' was the name famously given to psychoanalysis by one of Breuer's first patients, 'Anna O', and it is common to hear or read of the various forms of psychotherapy as 'talking treatments'. Such descriptions are of course true as far as they go but they are only part of the equation. They leave out what the philosopher Gemma Corradi Fiumara has felicitously called 'the other side of language', that is listening.[26]

It might seem absurd to suggest that psychotherapists ignore listening. Is this not, after all, precisely what we are engaged in all the time that we are working? The answer should be yes but the truth is that we take listening too much for granted and, through our own preconceptions, too often fail really to listen. We have a habit, as Heidegger remarked, of hearing only what we understand. This is particularly relevant to the practice of psychotherapy. Too often we hear only what we understand, what we have been trained to 'listen' for, what we tell ourselves is 'relevant' or 'important'.

So for instance one often hears psychotherapists in clinical discussions present material from sessions and one is struck by how much of what the patient says is skimmed over, as though it is of no importance. The therapist has been listening for what she believes is significant, usually something that confirms her speculations or hypotheses. Freud cautioned against this, of course, with his advocacy of 'evenly suspended attention', but like so much of Freud's practical advice, this is followed more in the breach than in the observance. Too often psychotherapists approach their work with a whole host of presuppositions, whether about the Oedipus complex, the depressive position, or indeed about life. We bring our mental maps into our consulting rooms, hoping they will help us to understand and make sense of what the patient says. And yet is this not a violence against the patient, something that gets in the way of *actually hearing what is said*? We cannot abandon all our presuppositions but we should be aware of them and attempt to suspend them. Only then can we be truly open to what is before us.

Talking presumes an interlocutor, a listener. Yet listening is little discussed within the discipline of psychotherapy. In this, it reflects the culture of which it is a part, a culture which, as Fiumara remarks, privileges expression, whether of the artist, the writer, the composer or orator. Listening on the other hand, Fiumara comments, belongs to the very essence of language but has no remunerative value. The stress in the dominant culture is always on the expressive capacity rather than the propensity to listen.[27] (Even Fiumara's own description, 'the other side', cannot but reflect this privileging of speech.)

Psychotherapy, as part of Western culture, privileges speaking. How often does one hear silence on the part of the psychotherapist described as 'passive', that she is engaged in 'just' listening? Listening, of course, does not preclude a speaking response. It would be a strange form of listening

72

which produced *only* silence. Attentive listening does not mean that the psychotherapist never – or even rarely – speaks. It is the quality of the listening that matters, not the quantity. But listening, while inevitably a precursor to speech, is not a means to an end, not a preparation for our own speech.

Speaking and listening are inextricably linked. Language, Levinas says, is 'above all the fact of being addressed . . . which means the saying much more than the said'.[28] I speak because I am being listened to. So too Bakhtin emphasised what he called the 'addressive quality' of ourselves, the fact that we address our own speech and acts in anticipation of the responses of others, real and imagined:

> In the actual life of speech every concrete act of understanding is active . . . and is indissolubly merged with the response, with a motivated agreement or disagreement. To some extent, primacy belongs to the response, as the activating principle; it creates the ground for understanding, it prepares the ground for an active and engaged understanding. Understanding comes to fruition only in the response. Understanding and response are dialectically merged and mutually condition each other; one is impossible without the other.[29]

Listening is not a 'technique' that can be taught. No amount of teaching, I suspect, can make of someone an attentive listener. It is rather an art or craft which can be developed only by practice. For Heidegger, listening is paying 'thoughtful attention to simple things';[30] for Bakhtin it is 'responsive understanding'; for Gadamer, 'Anyone who listens is fundamentally open. Belonging together always also means being able to listen to one another.'[31] So listening is a stance, a position, an attitude that we can choose to take – or not. And in order to listen we must really want to do it.

How then should we listen? It is impossible to lay down

73

rules. Perhaps a model for listening to speech is listening to music or, rather, how we should listen to music. Too often we 'listen' to music as background, as we do something else, while we are driving the car, cooking, reading a book or whatever. In this sense we are not really listening. But if we are attending to what we hear, without other distraction, and if we are truly open to what we hear, then we are listening. We are not trying to *understand* what we hear but, rather, are allowing ourselves to be touched by it – or indeed not touched by it – and surprised by it. A true listener hears not just the melody, what is most obvious, and is not distracted by this, but the many layers of sound that constitute the piece as a whole. A true listener hears, therefore, the conversations that go on within any piece. A listener who is trying to be true to what she is hearing does not compare what she is listening to with something else. At least she does not approach a piece in terms of what she is already familiar with, although such comparisons may suggest themselves in the process of listening. She is trying to hear the piece in its own terms, on its own ground.

> In authentically philo-sophical moments a part of our mind seems to remain suspended, 'passively' waiting for whatever expression might originate from a source that seems to be playing a more 'active' role. This *seeming* is due to our epistemic dislocation: it is in fact the 'passive' attitude of waiting that attracts and promotes the emergence of thought in the other. And it is in this demanding interaction of opposites that the process of genuine listening may unfold.[32]

By contrast there is, Fiumara warns, a pseudo-philosophy of listening that is not really *philo*-sophy because it is substantially colonising: 'This form of "listening" establishes at the outset that one of the two interlocutors dominates the interaction in terms of being able to better understand the other and the relationship itself.'[33] Similarly Gadamer remarks: 'The claim to understand the other person in advance performs the function of keeping the claim of the other at a distance.'[34]

The literature of psychotherapy is replete with examples which indicate the claim of 'understanding the other in advance'. Take, for instance, Melanie Klein's celebrated analysis of the young boy, Dick. The first time Klein meets Dick she gives him two trains which *she* designates 'Daddy-train' and 'Dick-train'. He rolls 'Dick-train' to the window and says, 'Station,' which prompts Klein to 'explain' that 'The station is Mummy; Dick is going into Mummy.' Dick leaves the train and runs between the inner and outer doors of the room, saying, 'Dark.' Again Klein 'explains' to him, 'It is dark inside Mummy. Dick is inside dark Mummy.'[35] These are just a few lines from a case study but they show clearly how it is Klein who is in charge of the situation and how she comes to this with a ready-made set of what *she* calls explanations. It is Klein who sets up the play by calling the trains 'Daddy' and 'Dick'. We have no way of knowing what Dick might have called them or how he would have seen them if left to his own devices (perhaps 'Spotty' and 'Dick'). Most important, there is not a shred of evidence in Dick's play *as described by Klein* that supports or even points to her 'explanation' that when Dick says, 'Station' he means his mother or that when he runs in the dark space between the doors he is somehow 'inside Mummy'. These so-called explanations or interpretations *come entirely* from Klein's preconceived theoretical system. That her statements may have had some effect on Dick as she claims do not in themselves *prove* their validity. A statement made by another, especially perhaps when one is in a state of some anxiety as Dick was, can have many meanings. It can indicate that the other is trying to communicate, that she is trying to understand; it may have a

75

reassuring quality of tone. Dick might well have felt that here was someone who was really trying to help him, who was engaging with him.

The meaning of a statement, in other words, is not limited to its content but is, rather, to be found in the total context, the total situation in which the two people find themselves. So when two people meet and begin to speak, the verbal content of what is said is only a part, and sometimes only a small part, of the conversation. Also present and to be attended to are such things as the social context of the conversation, the social relationship of the parties, the history of their relationship, their desires, their tones, modulations and gestures. How often do we hear, and not just in therapy, people recount an exchange or conversation which strikes them as simple or even insignificant, yet which has left them feeling a particular way, angry or upset for instance? And when we begin to look at what happened we see that it is anything but simple, that the parties had a history of some kind, that this was inescapably present when they met and that the 'real conversation' was going on unsaid, rather like the scene in Woody Allen's film *Annie Hall* where Allen's and Diane Keaton's thoughts about each other appear as subtitles and are seen to be quite different to the rather forced dialogue.

We listen not just to what is said, to the content, but to *how* something is said. Indeed, the distinction between content and tone is somewhat false. The two cannot readily be separated. Language is saturated with emotion. If it were not it would suggest that there was something like pure speech devoid of any emotive content altogether. This, of course, would be a nonsense. The meaning of a word is often indicated by tone. A simple word like 'Why?', for instance, means all sorts of things, exploration, interrogation, astonishment, despair, exasperation, aggression and so on, depending precisely on how it is said. For Bakhtin, tone – the least studied aspect of verbal life – is not defined by the objective content of the utterance, nor by the experiences of the speaker, but by the relation of the speaker to the person addressed.[36] Similarly Merleau-Ponty says that the emotional content of language, its 'gestural' sense, words, vowels, phonemes, are so many ways of 'singing' the world. Their function is to represent things not by reason of an objective resemblance, but because they extract, and literally express, their 'emotional essence'.[37]

In the context of psychotherapy the French philosopher and psychoanalyst Monique Schneider comments that violence has been done to the psychoanalytic *hearing* of the word when it follows Freud in distinguishing between the statement and the effect, as though the effect can only be understood as a quantity of emotion. When somebody speaks, Schneider says, 'what he says is the focus of attention, and the suffering in what he says . . . which penetrates everything that is said, is neglected.' Following Wittgenstein she reminds us that the suffering colours the whole of what is said and asks that intonation not be understood as a mode of seduction superimposed on the word but 'that which enables the understanding of the message itself', and allows us to rehear 'the breathing element in language of everything which is genuinely in the text – its energy, the many gestures of intimation'.[38]

But the other person is not the only thing to which we listen. We listen too to our own inner voice. As the great Polish film-maker, Andrzej Wajda, wrote, 'Every dialogue is made up not only of words but also silent reactions to those words, to our thoughts.'[39] These too are part of the dialogue of the conversation, the thoughts and the associations that are stirred up in us as we listen. Of course, we do not have to give voice to these but if we do not attend to them in some way we are missing something important. We are not fully participating in the conversation.

We listen also to our distractions and wanderings, not in the sense that these are somehow 'put into us' (projected) by the client, as one so often hears therapists say, but that they are part of what is going on *between* us. What do these tell us? Why, when I am with A, do I find myself thinking of my holidays, or with B wondering what I should make for dinner, or with C finding a particular song in my head? Why with D did I find that I had a sudden and unusual image? The more I practise psychotherapy, the more I come to trust or welcome these irruptions as telling me something, giving me clues, even if only potentially, about the person I am with and what is going on between us.

IN A SILENT WAY

> *Remember it is necessary to be aware*
> *Of every shape, of every kind of silence*
> *That slides past the making ear.*
> W. S. Graham[40]

As everyone knows or should know, in a conversation or dialogue we listen also to what is not said, the silences, the spaces in between the words, and yet there can be something frightening about silence, for the psychotherapist as much as the patient. The therapeutic conversation not only tolerates but welcomes silence, for it is in silence that all manner of things may emerge. As Walter Benjamin reminds us, 'to some degree all great texts contain their potential translation between the lines',[41] – a point underscored by the pianist Arthur Schnabel when he remarked, 'I don't think I handle the notes much differently from other pianists, but the pauses between the notes – ah, there is where the artistry lies.'[42] Ivan Illich goes so far as to say that it is not another's words that we have to understand so much as her silences if we want to understand her:

> To learn a language in a human and mature way, therefore, is to accept the responsibility for its silences and for its sounds ... A language of which I know only the words and not the pauses is a continuous offence. It is as the caricature of a photographic negative. The learning of the grammar of silence is an art much more difficult to learn than the grammar of sounds.[43]

Silence, Illich writes, has its pauses and hesitations, its rhythms and expressions and inflections, its durations and pitches, and times to be and not to be. As words must be learned by listening, so silences must be acquired by a 'delicate openness to them'.[44] To do this requires more time, delicacy and effort than it does to learn sounds.

Distinguishing types of silences, Illich says that first there is the silence of the pure listener, the silence through which the message of the other becomes 'he in us', the silence of deep interest. This silence, however, is threatened by another type of silence altogether, the silence of indifference which assumes that there is nothing that I want or can receive through the communication of the other.[45]

One must not, however, fetishise silence, as can happen. Remarking that the existentialists have made a myth out of silence, Agnes Heller reminds us that 'there is really no such thing as "silence": there are only concrete silence with concrete meaning.'[46]

> The dumb silence of apathy, the sober silence of solemnity, the fertile silence of awareness, the active silence of perception, the baffled silence of confusion, the uneasy silence of impasse, the muzzled silence of outrage, the expectant

silence of waiting, the reproachful silence of censure, the tacit silence of approval, the vituperative silence of accusation, the eloquent silence of awe, the unnerving silence of menace, the peaceful silence of communion, and the irrevocable silence of death illustrate by their unspoken responses to speech that experiences exist for which we lack the word.[47]

The point, as Heller says, is not to mystify silence. Rather we accept it, we think about it, we reflect on its possible meanings *at this moment* and we judge whether it is a silence that it is more beneficial, more fruitful to question or simply to let be, for the moment at least.

THE THERAPEUTIC CONVERSATION

Listening is part of dialogue, a word which David Bohm contrasts with the word discussion which has the same root as 'percussion' and 'concussion' and which really means to break things up. Discussion emphasises too the idea of analysis. A dialogue on the other hand 'is something more of a common participation, in which we are not playing a game against each other but *with* each other.' The object of dialogue is not to analyse or to win an argument or even to exchange opinions, 'Rather, it is to suspend your opinions and to look at the opinions – to listen to everybody's opinions, to suspend them, and to see what all that means.'[48]

The art of dialectic is not the art of being able to win every argument. On the contrary, it is possible that someone who is practising the art of dialectic, i.e. the art of questioning and seeking truth, comes off worse in the argument in the eyes of those listening to it. Dialectic, as the art of asking questions, proves itself only because the person who knows how to ask questions is able to persist in the questioning, which involves being able to preserve his orientation towards openness.[49]

Dialogue does not mean, as is so often thought, a two-sided conversation. Rather it means, *through* language. In other words, it is through language that meaning emerges. In the particular language game that is psychotherapy anything and everything is appropriate. Yet, how often does one encounter patients who feel they should speak only of certain things, who believe that there are correct and incorrect, appropriate or inappropriate matters for the therapeutic session? So too does one hear psychotherapists complain about things patients say or who pass over things they do not regard as important. Such patients, it is said, do not know that they should not ask questions, or pass personal remarks about the psychotherapist and so on. And yet it is precisely in these moments of supposed in appropriateness that one can come closer to the truth of a person and of their encounter with us.

It was Freud, apparently, who described psychoanalysis as an 'ordinary conversation' (according to J.-B. Pontalis) and so it should be in the sense that our language should be that of the everyday. And yet in many ways it is an *extra*ordinary conversation. It is primarily concerned with one party to the conversation – the other, not me; it is bounded by space and time, although these parameters vary among therapists; it not only tolerates silence but welcomes it, in a way that would be thought odd in most other contexts; and the normal conventions of conversation and social behaviour can be suspended in that the patient can, if she is so moved, be angry, aggressive, sulky, withdrawn, contemptuous, prejudiced, flirtatious, provocative and so on without risk of criticism, condemnation or retaliation.

In the world of psychotherapy, no one has emphasised the ordinary nature of the therapeutic conversation more con-

vincingly than Peter Lomas. If we want to get to know someone, Lomas says, and this is surely what psychotherapy is about,
then we should feel free to do this in whatever ways feel right
to us, 'the tentative, risky, tactful, revealing, confronting and
innumerable other attitudes that go along the path to intimacy'.[50] For a long time I worried that I asked too many
questions of people in therapy. But surely this is one of the
ways we find out about people – what they think of something
they have mentioned, what they feel, how they make sense of
a habit or inclination, what they are thinking when silent and
so on. Of course, questions can be intrusive; therapy is not an
interrogation and one must know when to keep silent.

I said above that the therapeutic conversation is one that is
primarily concerned with one party – the patient. What then
of the much-dreaded 'self-revelation', of answering questions?
While I do not believe that volunteering information about
oneself is useful to the therapeutic process and can become
abusive – the therapy is, after all, the patient's – the much-
vaunted anonymity of the therapist seems to me questionable.
For a start, just how anonymous can one really be? The kind
of house I live in, the area in which it is located, the clothes I
wear, the way I speak, the manner in which I comport myself,
the taste (or lack of it) that I show in the room in which I
work – all these say a great deal about me. In addition, the
psychotherapy world is a small one and it is hard to avoid
hearing about others in it. The point I am making here is not,
however, whether anonymity is possible – one could if one so
wished go to great lengths to ensure a greater degree – but
whether it is desirable. I have come to believe that it may be
helpful for the patient to know certain things that she wishes
to know. Answering a question honestly in no way precludes
exploring what that question means to the questioner, nor
what it means to be given the information sought. Of course,
one must decide for oneself what one is happy disclosing and
know when to draw the line but a certain candour is necess-

ary if one wishes to engage in a meaningful dialogue or conversation with another. What we might call the tease of therapy – the enigmatic therapist who appears as a blank screen – can have as much to do with maintaining a position of therapeutic power as it has with any theoretical justification.

The therapeutic conversation is, it seems to me, much more like an ordinary conversation than we might like to believe. That we do not want to believe it stems, to be sure, from an adherence to a different understanding of psychotherapy from the one proposed here, but it has to do also with questions of power and status. If we are, to a considerable extent, engaged in an ordinary conversation then much of the privileged status and power that accrues to us by virtue of specialist knowledge melts into air. But what then of interpretation, it might be asked? Is this not the task of the therapist?

The place of interpretation in psychotherapy seems to me to be greatly exaggerated. Interpretations, as Charles Rycroft has pointed out, are after all only one class of statements that psychotherapists make to their patients. Others involve greetings and farewells, the formal arrangements of the therapy; they draw attention to recurrent themes, inconsistencies or omissions, and they explain general ideas, such as ambivalence.[51] So too the word interpretation has been stretched to become meaningless. A great many of what psychotherapists call interpretations are not that at all. Frequently they are repetitions of what the patient has said, sometimes rephrased, similar to what some therapists call 'reflecting'. So too many so-called interpretations are summations of what the patient has been talking about, often involving an attempt to draw out a particular theme. This is not to criticise such practices, which have their place in therapy, but they should not be designated interpretations. That they are so designated seems to me related to our desire as psychotherapists to be seen as experts. We feel the need to *do* something and this something is interpretation. It is this that marks out our expertise, this that distinguishes us from the non-therapist, including the patient.

More important is Charles Rycroft's observation that the impact of interpretations cannot be attributed solely to the intellectual content of what is said. Even when it is free of reassurance or suggestion, Rycroft says, every correct interpretation

> contains within it a whole number of additional implicit communications about the analyst and his attitude towards the patient. In addition to enlightening the patient about, say, his fantasies or defences, it also indicates that the analyst is still present and awake, that he has been listening and has understood what the patient has been talking about, that he remembers what the patient has said during the present and previous sessions – and that he has been sufficiently interested to listen and remember and understand.[52]

The interpretation, in other words, tells the patient that the therapist is interested in her as another human being and that it is possible to have a relationship with another person without violation or distortion of her own subjective experience and intrinsic capacity for growth.[53] I believe that the ancillary significance of the interpretation is rather more important than even Rycroft considered it. Indeed I wonder if this isn't more important than what the therapist actually says, a point made by Winnicott who observed that 'What matters to the patient is not the accuracy of the interpretation so much as the willingness of the analyst to help, the analyst's capacity to identify with the patient and so to believe in what is needed and to meet the need as soon as the need is indicated verablly or in non-verbal or pre-verbal language.'[54]

Language, dialogue, conversation – these are matters far

more complex than we normally take them to be. It is through them that we are constituted as human beings, as part of the human community, and through them that we come not just to know each other and ourselves, but to be with each other, although this being with is always a process, never a complete state, and may also be only a possibility.

4

Waiting, witnessing
and naming

*The witness testifies to what has been said
through him. Because the witness has said, 'here
I am' before the other.*

Emmanuel Levinas[1]

Whatever else we may do as psychotherapists we wait – we
wait for, we wait with and we wait upon those who come to
see us; we wait and we witness. What does this mean, to wait
or to witness?

WAITING OR 'THE ART OF UNKNOWING'[2]

*The language of awaiting – perhaps it is silent,
but it does not separate speaking and silence; it
makes of silence already a kind of speaking;
already it says in silence the speaking that silence
is. For mortal silence does not keep still.*

Maurice Blanchot[3]

In an ethical therapy we wait upon the patient. This idea of
waiting upon or attendance is part of the meaning of the
Greek word *therapeia* which, as Joe Friedman has written,
meant most commonly 'service' or 'attendance', particularly

of persons to the gods, but also to parents, children, animals and plants. A second meaning was that of 'medical treatment or cure'.[4] The practice of *therapeia*, Friedman says, was to witness a constant call to a larger Being and be in accord with it.[5]

Contrast this, Friedman suggests, with technology. 'Service has to do with attending to the goals, aims, problematics and questions raised by that which is to be served (whether that be a game, a piece of music, a friendship, and so on). It has as part of its structure a concern with boundaries (What is to be served?) rather than goals other than those given to us by what is to be served.'[6]

But what, in therapy, is it that we wait for? Just as waiting is to be found in the word therapy, so is it inscribed in the word patient that is sometimes used in therapy, one who waits, who endures. But waiting is also what is called for from the therapist. To wait *for* something in therapy is, it seems to me, to have already prejudged the situation, to have imposed one's own view on the other of what ought to happen. If one waits for something, one has a purpose in mind or rather one has imposed a purpose on the patient and on the therapy. It is a violence against the other.

Of course, it is difficult, in our culture, to imagine that we do not wait *for* anything. This is so antithetical to our customary ways of being and thinking. In so many situations we wait *for* something. In everyday life we wait for a bus or train, we wait for a friend to arrive, a phone call, a letter. In our cultural lives too we wait for things. We wait for 'something' to happen in a film, in a story or a piece of music. We have become so accustomed to what we call plot development, and speedy plot development at that, that we become impatient with anything that refuses to move on, that wishes to linger and wishes for us to linger with it. The film that wishes to takes its time and wishes for us to take our time with it, the cinema of, for instance, Angelopoulos, Antonioni,

Ozu, Tarkovsky and the earlier Wim Wenders, has become almost unimaginable today, an object of dismissal and ridicule. Wenders himself has commented:

> When people think they've seen enough of something, but there's more, and no change of shot, then they react in a curiously livid way. They think there must be some justification for it, but it never occurs to them that the fact that you happen to like whatever is in the shot is sufficient justification. They imagine there has to be some other reason, and when they can't find it they get mad. It makes them madder than when a film actually insults them – which can happen too.[7]

So too in music. Much of the work of twentieth-century composers such as Olivier Messiaen, Morton Feldman and others marked a break with the idea, so firmly rooted in (Western) musical culture, of a necessary 'development' in pieces of music. Such music, as the critic Andrew Clements has written of Messiaen's, 'does not strive for a goal like a great romantic symphony; it suspends time and exists in its own wonderstruck contemplative world'. It does not seek movement from A to B to C according to predetermined rules or conventions, but rather is concerned with the creation of space or mood.[8]

Waiting is, of course, inextricably linked to the idea of attention, as the French makes clear: there is *l'attention* (attention) and *l'attente* (waiting). A beautiful passage by Blanchot about attention is germane to what we do in psychotherapy:

> Attention *is* waiting; not the effort, the tension or the mobilization of knowledge around something with which one might concern oneself. Attention waits. It waits without precipitation, leaving empty what is empty and keeping

our haste, our impatient desire, and, even more, our horror
of emptiness from prematurely filling it in. Attention is the
emptiness of thought oriented by a gentle force and maintained in an accord with the empty intimacy of time.[9]

Commenting on this passage, Zygmunt Bauman reminds us –
in words that seem to me especially appropriate to the
practice of psychotherapy – that such waiting is not possess-
ive; it does not aim at dispossessing the other of his will, of
his distinctiveness and identity, either through physical coer-
cion or the intellectual conquest called 'the definition'. Proximity is neither a distance bridged, nor a distance demanding
to be bridged; it is not a preamble to identification and
merger. Rather, proximity is content to be just that, proximity, 'the state of permanent attention come what may.'[10]
In the world of psychotherapy no one has advocated a
more radical approach to waiting than W. R. Bion. Bion
encapsulated his approach when he enjoined therapists to
approach sessions 'without memory or desire', a remark
which is frequently quoted, only then to be warned against or
just simply ignored. Bion elaborated on this in his remarkable
seminars and conversations:

In every consulting room there ought to be two rather
frightened people: the patient and the psychoanalyst. If they
are not, one wonders why they are bothering to find out
what everyone knows. It is tempting always to engage upon
something familiar. This temptation is greater for psychoanalysts than for others because it is one of the rare situations in which human beings can be engaged in a frightening occupation without even going outside the door.[11]

Discard your memory; discard the future tense of your
desire; forget them both, both what you knew and what
you want, to leave space for a new idea. A thought, an idea

unchained, may be floating around the room searching for a home. Amongst these may be one of your own which seems to turn up from your insides, or one from outside yourself, namely the patient.[12]

The more one is occupied with what one wants to happen and with what happened, or what one knows about the patient or psychoanalysis, the less space is left for uncertainty. If I become more and more dogmatic, and more and more sure that the patient said this, that or the other to me last time, I know I must be getting tired. When we are tired we find it difficult to be receptive. The actor has to learn to articulate so that he is audible at the beginning and at the end of a performance. The analyst has to be receptive and sensitive at the end of the session as well as at the beginning.[13]

So too Winnicott wrote, in 1971, that it was only after forty years of working as a psychoanalyst that he had become able to wait and wait for the natural evolution of the transference arising out of the patient's growing trust, and to avoid breaking up this process by interpretation.

If only we can wait the patient arrives at understanding creatively and with immense joy, and now I enjoy this joy more than I used to enjoy the sense of having been clever. I think I interpret mainly to let the patient know the limits of my understanding.[14]

It sometimes seems as though none of this had ever been written. Too often, psychotherapists suffer from what the American psychoanalyst Stephen Kurtz aptly calls a 'compulsion to make sense'. Kurtz says that he uses the word compulsion rather than effort, for more than mere misguidedness is at work: 'To experience the patient's words openly, without passing them through a pre-formed cognitive screen, can occasion great anxiety. The defences erected against this anxiety have found institutional expression in analytic theory and practice. In so doing, they are instances of a greater fear of unknowing that pervades the Western mind. The compulsion to make sense will only hold attunement back, leaving the patient misunderstood, isolated and unloved.'[15] Again this was something understood by Bion who said, 'If I spend the time trying to understand what you are telling me, then I cannot listen to you.'[16] So too, he said, memories and desires hid what was going on. 'This, I believe, is equally true of understanding.'[17]

The compulsion to make sense, Kurtz says, 'is a resistance to unknowing'.[18] The analyst, Kurtz argues, usually has not analysed his addiction to the analytic role, the addiction to understanding and the 'cohesion-producing functions' (e.g. through offering interpretations and weaving narratives) which is a route to power not just over the other person, but more importantly over his own discomfort with unstructured experience. 'Can the analyst', Kurtz asks, 'allow the patient to cure him of this need [to understand] and to open up a world that does not make sense?'[19]

This radical advocacy of unknowing is akin to the theological idea of the *via negativa*, or negative way. This is the belief, present in the teachings of the Gnostics of formative Christianity, in the impossibility of knowing or describing God directly. It was the inspiration for many notable mystics such as the anonymous fourteenth-century English author of 'The Cloud of Unknowing' and St John of the Cross who called it 'the dark night of the soul'. The video artist Bill Viola, who links it to his own creative processes, describes it in this way:

The basic tenets of the *via negativa* are the unknowability of God; that God is wholly other, independent, complete, that God cannot be grasped by the human intellect, cannot be described in any way; that when the mind faces the divine reality, it becomes blank. It seizes up. It enters a cloud of unknowing. When the eyes cannot see, then the only thing to go on is faith, and the only way to approach God is within . . . the essence here is the individual faith . . .[20]

One does not need to be religious to appreciate the relevance of such a belief to the practice of psychotherapy or indeed to other fields. Viola writes of himself: 'I relate to the role of the mystic in the sense of following a *via negativa* – of feeling the basis of my work to be in unknowing, in doubt, in being lost, in questions and not answers – and that recognising that personally the most important work I have done has come from not knowing what I was doing at the time I was doing it.'[21]

This is what the sixteenth-century Christian mystic St John of the Cross had in mind when he wrote:

> To come to the knowledge you have not
> You must go by a way in which you know not.[22]

Or as T. S. Eliot would paraphrase it in 'East Coker':

> In order to arrive at what you do not know
> You must go by a way which is a way of ignorance . . .;
> . . . And what you do not know is the only thing you know.[23]

This idea has found its way into discussions of literary creativity. It is, for example, what Keats meant by 'negative capability':

> I had not a dispute but a disquisition with Dilke on various subjects; several things dove-tailed in my mind, and at once

it struck me what quality went to form a Man of Achieve-ment, especially in Literature, and which Shakespeare pos-sessed so enormously – I mean Negative Capability, that is, when a man is capable of being in uncertainties, mysteries, doubts, without any irritable reaching after fact and reason.[24]

A similar point was made by Coleridge:

I warn all Inquirers into this hard point to *wait* – not only not to plunge forward before the Word is *given* to them, but not even to paw the ground with impatience. For in a deep stillness only can this truth be apprehended.[25]

All these writers and artists point to the same truth. If you want to know something, in the sense of artistic or creative truth, you cannot just set out to find it. Knowing is not something that can be willed. It can only be hoped for. One must wait. It is *only* by waiting that one can allow something new and surprising to emerge. This waiting requires a giving up – of expectations, hopes, wishes and, perhaps above all, of a desire to understand what one is faced with. (One does not have to be a creative artist to appreciate this. We can see it in the most mundane ways. Many if not most people will have had, at some time or another, the experience of grasping something or obtaining something they desire seemingly with-out effort, by being open to possibility.)

Let us, here and now, dispose of the notion of 'passivity' in therapy. One sometimes hears therapists say in a derogatory, or at least critical, way that such and such a therapist is 'passive'. He is not intervening 'enough' (whatever that may mean); he is too silent. Often this betrays a misunderstanding of the word. To be passive, in its most common usage, is to allow things to be done to one. We use it as the opposite of active. But in therapy what is sometimes called being passive

93

is a waiting and an allowing and an attending. It is a
menifestation of respect for the patient and of responsibilty
to him. In this sense waiting is, perhaps, a *radical* passivity in
the sense suggested by Blanchot when he writes:

> 'Be patient'. A simple motto, very demanding. Patience has
> already withdrawn me not only from the will in me, but
> from my power to be patient: if I *can* be patient, then
> patience has not worn out in me that me to which I cling
> for self-preservation. Patience opens me entirely, all the
> way to a passivity which is the *pas* [not] in the utterly
> passive, and which has therefore abandoned the level of life
> where *passive* would simply be the opposite of *active*.[26]

There is, as Blanchot says, an inattention which is disdainful
insensitivity. But there is the more passive inattention which,
'beyond any interest or calcuation, *lets others be other*,
leaving them outside the sphere of the violence by which they
would be caught, grasped, snared, identified, reduced to
sameness'.[27]

Psychotherapy then, whatever else it may be, is a lesson in
waiting for both patient and psychotherapist. Both may
require the lesson: the patient who is in a hurry for the result,
for a solution, albeit understandably, and the therapist who
is in a rush to understand and make sense. Such waiting is of
course constantly being undermined by a culture which wants
results and wants them speedily. In the world of psychotherapy this is illustrated by the increasing popularity of
forms of brief or time-limited therapies. These have their
place but they should not be allowed to undermine the place
of time-unlimited therapy, not as some kind of luxury but as
a necessity.

THE ACT OF WITNESSING

> *To be a witness, try to remember.*
> *That cannot be done.*
>   Czeslaw Milosz[28]

In our benighted century, the century of the death camps and of the Gulag, the witnessing of historical trauma has become established as an important literary form as well as a function of historical memory. If it has one exemplar it is undoubtedly the Italian Jewish chemist, Primo Levi, survivor of Auschwitz, whose many books dare to speak of the unspeakable and testify to the horror he endured. Other important witnesses would include Victor Serge, Nadezhda Mandelstam, Eugenia Ginzburg, Bruno Bettelheim, Jorge Semprun, Eduardo Galeano, Binyamin Wilkomirski, Jung Chang. Their and others' writings have spoken movingly, sometimes unbearably, not only of the terrible times through which they have lived but of the many human responses to such happenings.[29] Such witnessing was defined by the revolutionary socialist writer, Victor Serge, who probably has a claim to being the first in this line, as 'a means of expressing for people what most of them live without being able to express, as a means of communion, as a testimony about the vast life that flows through us and whose essential aspect we must try to fix for the benefit of those who will come after us.'[30] Witnessing is, in other words, an act of solidarity and community, something which connects us to other human beings and which, above all, testifies to the truths of life.

But here we must recall Primo Levi's own remark that the real witnesses had not survived:

> ... we, the survivors, are not the true witnesses. We survivors are not only an exiguous but also an anomalous

minority: we are those who, by their prevarications or
abilities or good luck did not touch bottom. Those who did
so, those who saw the Gorgon, have not returned to tell
about it, or have remained mute . . . They are the rule, we
are the exception.[31]

The importance of witnessing in psychotherapy came to me
when I was seeing for therapy people who had been tortured
or subjected to other forms of institutionalised violence, what
we have come to know in shorthand as 'ethnic cleansing'.
What, in the face of their accounts, could I possibly say that
was of any meaning? What, in such circumstances, was the
relevance of any 'interpretation' that I might have made?
What such situations called for, it gradually became clear to
me, was an act of witnessing, of attentiveness and of acceptance. (It is difficult to use the word given not just its religious
associations but also its quasi-religious associations, such as
is found in the psychotheraputic dogma of the therapist as
witness to the suffering 'child within' or the 'inner child'.)
The prisoners in Auschwitz, Primo Levi recalled, had a recur-
ring nightmare. It was that they survived the death camp and
returned home, only for no one to believe what had happened
to them:

> It is an intense pleasure, physical, inexpressible, to be at
> home, among friendly people and to have so many things
> to recount: but I cannot help noticing that my listeners do
> not follow me. In fact, they are completely indifferent: they
> speak confusedly of other things among themselves, as if I
> was not there. My sister looks at me, gets up and goes
> away without a word.[32]

Levi himself was to find this dream or nightmare come true
when he wrote his first book about his experience and could

find no major publisher willing to take it on. A small publisher did so but the book quickly went out of print.

But witnessing is not limited to people who have experienced such historical traumas although it is particularly relevant to them. It is an intrinsic part of *any* therapeutic process. Indeed, it is part of what makes therapy therapeutic.

What then is it to witness? It is to listen, to hear, to receive but to do so in a particular way. If we are listening only in order to 'translate' or interpret what is being said are we not guilty of doing violence to what is said? It is also to believe. Witnessing does not preclude interpretation or exploration, which may be appropriate, although it should go without saying that tact and timing are of the essence. Sometimes, though, there is simply nothing to be said. Indeed, we are not called upon to say anything. It is sufficient that we listen, that we attend. Indeed, it is precisely this silent witnessing that is called for from us. Witnessing is being present in a particular way, a co-presencing. When we say in common parlance that someone is a good listener, if we mean anything other than that they remain silent when we speak, we refer to this. We feel we have been heard and in some sense understood even if we have been offered no advice. Of course, it will be said that psychotherapy is more than this. And, of course, it is, but it cannot take place without this kind of attentiveness, a kind of attentiveness which is all too often absent.

There is in psychotherapy a double witnessing. There is the witnessing of the patient who speaks of, testifies to his suffering, trauma, pain or dilemmas. But the psychotherapist is, in turn, witness to this. 'The testimony to the trauma', Dori Laub writes, 'thus includes its hearer, who is, so to speak, the blank screen on which the event comes to be inscribed for the first time.' It is in this process of double witnessing that 'the knowing of the event is given birth to.

The listener, therefore, is a party to the creation of knowledge *de novo*.'[33] Indeed, Laub's co-author Shoshana Felman reminds us that the testimony should be understood not as a *statement* of truth but rather as a *mode of access* to that truth. In the act of speaking and of being listened to and attended to, the witness not only witnesses, but begets truth.[34] Knowledge in the testimony is not a factual given that is reproduced by the person testifying, but rather 'a genuine advent, an event in its own right'.[35] It is something creative. Something new emerges. The 'facts' may be the same but they become emotionally charged and hence changed. The therapist who witnesses addresses the rending and forsaken cry of the poet Paul Celan, survivor of German forced labour and like Primo Levi a suicide in later years, who wrote at a particularly besieged time in his life:

> No one
> witnesses for the
> witness.[36]

Witnessing is not a 'stage' in the process of psychotherapy or even a stage in a session, something which precedes or even follows something else. Rather we might think of it as a moment in therapy and, as such, something that is ever present or which recurs. It may occur at the beginning of a therapeutic process, or at the end, or anywhere in between. It may be how a session begins or how it ends or, again, anywhere in between. Indeed, there is a sense in which even when we are offering an interpretation or intervening in some other way, we may still be engaged in an act of witnessing – that is, witnessing occurs simultaneously with anything else the therapist may do. It is ever present.

NAMING

'If you can't name, you're not human,' says the narrator of E. L. Doctorow's novella, *Lives of the Poets*, worried that he is losing his mind.[37] So too in Gabriel Garcia Marquez's imagined village of Macondo, the alchemist Aureliano Buendia, in an attempt to combat the impact of the insomnia plague, labels everything in his laboratory. Then his father imposes the practice upon the whole village:

> With an inked brush he marked everything with its name: *table, chair, clock, door, wall, bed, pan.* He went to the corral and marked the animals and plants: *cow, goat, pig, hen, cassava, caladium, banana.*

But Jose Arcadio Buendia then realises that labelling is not enough:

> . . . he realised that the day might come when things would be recognised by their inscriptions but that no one would remember their use. Then he was more explicit. The sign that he hung on the neck of the cow was an exemplary proof of the way in which the inhabitants of Macondo were prepared to fight against the loss of memory: *This is the cow. She must be milked every morning so that she will produce milk, and the milk must be boiled in order to be mixed with coffee to make coffee and milk.* Thus they went on living in a reality that was slipping away, momentarily captured by words, but which would escape irremediably when they forgot the value of the written letters.[38]

One of the things we do in psychotherapy is to name things. A great deal of confusion is caused through the inability of people to name what it is they are feeling and to distinguish one emotion from another. Despite the growth of therapy and 'the triumph of the therapeutic', in Philip Rieff's nice phrase, we inhabit a culture marked by what Susie Orbach has called 'emotional illiteracy'. We can, most of us, read and write. More books are published than ever before. Even very young children are computer literate. We have access to more information than ever before. And yet, to a considerable extent, we remain helpless before our emotions, unable to know what they are, to put names to them:

> Emotional illiteracy exists because we have no shared language for emotional life. Words like love, hate, jealousy and competition reveal little more than the tip of an emotional experience whose depths we are unused to exploring. When we try to talk about feelings . . . we both feel and engender shame and embarrassment. When we try to create a new language, a way of telling, we face scorn for speaking psychobabble. But while psychobabble is an ugly and cheap way to solve the problem of putting inchoate feelings into words, the scorn expresses our culture's fear of the emotional. Language has for many of us been a way of hiding our feelings.[39]

The importance of naming has been articulated by several poets. In 'the no man's land of the nameless,' the Hungarian poet Ágnes Nemes Nagy has written, 'it is the duty of the poet to obtain citizenship for an increasing horde of Nameless emotions'.[40] For Paul Celan, about whom I shall say more later, poetry 'names and composes' and in doing so 'tries to measure out the sphere of the given and the possible'.[41] So it is one of the tasks of the psychotherapist to help the patient name his emotions, to give them language. Naming is a way of orienting ourselves in the world, a way of finding our place and our way. As I have said, a great deal of confusion is caused by people not knowing what their feelings are. We latch on to catch-all words or phrases – depressed is a common one, a word that says a lot and at the same time almost nothing – and it can be a revelation to people to know that they have feelings and that they have names: loss, sadness, despair, fear, terror, anger, rage, joy, love and so on. This emotional confusion causes great difficulties as people act out what they feel rather than struggling to know it and come terms to with it. Look around us and we see this everywhere – it is there in the virtual epidemic of eating disorders and alcohol and drug abuse; it is there in the violence of the home, the city centres, the school playground; it is there in anything we choose to label anti-social. It was part of Winnicott's genius that he could, in his consultations with parents and children, put names to things that were troubling them or help others put names to them. So therapy is in part a learning about the language of the emotions, not in some sense of being instructed or told – there are few things worse in this regard than hearing people mouth a learned language of feelings that is not theirs, a language *about* feeling but devoid *of* feeling – but in the true sense of the word, of a drawing out of something that is there, of fostering a capacity. Of course it is not enouogh simply to put a name on things, to label, as the people of Macondo realised. Naming is not an end but a beginning. The word or phrase is the start of, or a point in, the process of exploration of meaning.

While seeking to name we must also be wary of the danger of naming, in particular the idea that in naming something we think we have 'got it', have fixed it like a butterfly pinned upon a board. Naming in this sense can be destructive of that which is named. This is something that the Jewish tradition has always recognised in its injunction against the naming of God. If we name God, then we limit him and render him 'less than'. We can see the dangers of naming at work from the other side of psychotherapy, as it were, in the tendency of therapists to name conditions or syndromes, to use diagnostic categories when speaking of patients. We say someone is neurotic, hypochondriac, hysterical, psychotic, obsessional and so on and feel that we are saying something meaningful about the person concerned. So too some names have become clichés, emptied of meaning through overuse. Envy would be one such, anxiety perhaps another. It is not that these do not exist but that the words lose their meaning. Our task then is to rename, redescribe. True, such words can describe 'constellations' to use Walter Benjamin's word, clusters of terms and images whose mutual affinity creates a space from within which the particular can emerge,[42] and can serve as a kind of shorthand among colleagues, but they can too easily lead us into thinking that we actually know something or more than we really do.

CONCLUSION

Let me repeat, there is nothing 'passive', at least in the ordinary, usually derogatory sense of the word, in what I am advocating. Waiting, witnessing and naming all require a great deal of effort on the part of the therapist, albeit an effort of restraint, of toleration, of withstanding demands by the patient. Nor am I advocating silence – although there are times when there is nothing to be said and such times have to be respected. Waiting in particular does not mean doing nothing. There are many ways in which one waits.

5

'A dwelling in the evening air': the place of therapy

Home
A sort of honour, not a building site,
Wherever we are, when if we choose, we might
Be somewhere else, but trust that we have chosen right.

W. H. Auden[1]

Man's relation to locations, and through loca-
tions to spaces, inheres in his dwelling. The
relationship between man and space is none other
than dwelling, strictly thought and spoken.

Martin Heidegger[2]

Man does not live by words alone; all 'subjects'
are situated in a space in which they must recog-
nise themselves or lose themselves, a space which
they may both enjoy and modify.

Henri Lefebvre[3]

The language of psychotherapy is replete with spatial meta-phors. Environment, container, holding, a secure base, the setting, the frame – these are just some of the metaphorical or figurative ways in which therapy is described. Despite this, it is surprising that we attend so little to the fact that we are spatial beings, beings situated in physical space, *embodied*. (It is not that I have a body, but that I *am* my body, as Merleau-Ponty reminds us.) So too is it surprising that we attend little to the nature of the therapeutic space, to the fact that therapy has to *take place somewhere*. What is the nature of this place, this somewhere? I shall come to this actual place in due course but I want first to attend to place in a more metaphorical sense.

Whatever else it might be called, the twentieth century might be thought of as the century of homelessness. As at no time before, millions of people are homeless or dislocated from home, through war, famine, economic exploitation, environmental destruction or whatever. So too has migration for work become for millions of people a hallmark of economic life. But this physical homelessness has coincided with another form or dimension of homelessness, a homelessness of the spirit. Humans in modern times, prominent sociologists can write, are affected by '*a deepening condition of "home-lessness"* . . . a metaphysical loss of home', a condition, they comment, that has been psychologically hard to bear and has engendered its own nostalgias, that is for a condition of being at home, in oneself and in the universe.[4]

This longing for a home is not, as some postmodernists can imply, some sort of pathology, the search for a *heimat* some kind of fantasy. Although it may take objectionable forms, as in extreme nationalism or racism, the longing for a home, the need for a home are, one is tempted to say, basic human drives. There is not a human being alive who does not need a home of some kind, a sense of belonging. The nomad carries her sense of this belonging with her. Home is our centre of orientation in the world, an originary place from which we explore and discover the world beyond. Remember, says Bachelard, that 'man is laid in the cradle of house' before he is ' "cast into the world", as claimed by certain hasty meta-physics'. The house is the human being's first world and without it she would be a dispersed being.[5]

'A dwelling in the evening air': the place of therapy

And yet home is not what it once was. The fundamentally changed meaning of home has been well articulated by Agnes Heller in answer to her own question, 'Where are we at home?' In earlier times, Heller writes, the 'things of the everyday habitat' provided constancy in periods of dramatic and painful transformation:

> Napoleon's grand army invaded Europe, yet the same watch was inherited from the grandfather by the father and from the father to the son. Not just the mansions of the English gentry but the cottages of the French peasants remained populated by the same things. When the son returned home from his wanderings, he would find everything at its old place, even if their historical lustre was sometimes gone.[6]

What has been described as the second work of Western literature, Homer's *Odyssey*, is concerned with precisely this, Odysseus' return home to Ithaca from the Trojan war. His home is where it was and how it was and, although surrounded by suitors, Penelope his wife waits for him, along with his son Telemachus. In our own century, in the wake of the Holocaust and the Gulag, this is no longer the case: 'The son who now returns from his wanderings, will not recognise the home of his childhood. There is still remembrance without the possibility of recognition.' Hence the rise of nostalgia in its myriad forms. Hence too some of the passion found in ecological movements. 'The protection of the environment is also the protection of the home, the habitat where one could still return'.[7]

In any case, we have come increasingly to ask whether our experience of home was a good one, to be sceptical of our memories:

> Home sweet home – but is it so sweet, or has it been so sweet? The familiar fragrance can be the smell of burning

105

flesh. The familiar gesture can be the hand raised to beat. The colour can be dark and grey. Home is where we were weeping, but no one listened, where we were hungry and cold. Home was the small circle one could not break through, the childhood that seemed endless, the tunnel without exit. It was, after all, in a world where we all had a home where the metaphor of the earth as the valley of tears so fully described our experience. How good not to return, not even on the couch of the analyst.[8]

As individuals, in other words, we do not feel at home. Our place and position – in the world and in ourselves – are insecure, shaky as perhaps never before. (Whether the security of the past was a myth or fiction is not the point here.) Hence, as Heller and others point out, the pull of nostalgia, that search for the world we have lost. Hence too the attraction of extreme forms of nationalism and neo-tribalism, to borrow Michael Walzer's apt description. In each can be seen the search for a place to belong, for an end to homelessness.

While some seek a home in movements of this kind and the political project of nationalism, a more personal, individual sense of homelessness, of unbelonging, is also what brings many people to therapy. People seek therapy because in very particular and precise ways they are not at home with themselves or with others. (The exact nature of this 'not at homeness' is, of course, crucial and will be, inevitably, much of the stuff of the therapy.) We do not, we cannot, *make* people feel at home, but in the place of therapy they may, hopefully will, come to feel more at home in themselves and in the world. Familiarity, writes Agnes Heller, is a matter of being accustomed:

Familiarity provides the basis for our everyday activities, and at the same time it is an everyday need. Integral to the average everyday life is awareness of a fixed point in space, a firm position from which we 'proceed' . . . and to which we return in due course. This firm position is what we call 'home'.[9]

Now, as Heller goes on to say, home is not just a matter of a roof over one's head and a family. People may have these but have no home. Familiarity is not equivalent to being at home but it is an indisputable ingredient.

> Over and above this, we need the feeling of confidence: 'home' protects us. We also need the intensity and density of human relations, the warmth of the home. 'Going home' should mean returning to that firm position which we know, to which we are accustomed, where we feel safe, and where our emotional relationships are at their most intense.[10]

Such familiarity is not a given but an achievement. To return to Levinas, the home is not like other possessable goods but is possessed precisely *because it is hospitable*. This hospitality, moreover, is an accomplishment.[11] (Levinas's *Totality and Infinity*, Derrida remarks, can be read as an immense treatise on hospitality.) Home, as Levinas writes, is 'not an indifferent "somewhere", but a base, a condition.'[12] The privileged role of the home does not consist in being the end of human activity but in being its condition, its commencement:

> Man abides in the world as having come to it from a private domain, from being at home with himself, to which at each moment he can retire . . . Simultaneously without and within, he goes forth outside from an inwardness . . . the subject contemplating a world presupposes the event of

107

dwelling, the withdrawal from the elements (that is, from immediate enjoyment, already uneasy about the morrow), recollection in the intimacy of the home.[13]

Home, as Eliot puts it in 'East Coker', is where one *starts* from.[14]

This familiarity or dwelling is in itself existence. 'To exist', Levinas says, 'means to dwell, in the sense of a recollection, a coming to oneself, a retreat home with oneself as in a land of refuge . . .'[15] So too for Heidegger who links dwelling etymologically to being. The old German word, *bauen*, to which *ich bin* (I am) belongs, means to dwell. 'The way in which you are and I am,' says Heidegger, 'the manner in which we humans *are* on the earth, is Buan, dwelling. To be a human being means to be on the earth as a mortal. It means to dwell.'[16]

For Heidegger, the real plight of dwelling does not lie merely in a lack of houses: 'The real dwelling plight lies in this, that mortals ever search anew for the nature of dwelling, that they *must ever learn to dwell*. What if man's homelessness consisted in this, that man still does not even think of the *real* plight of dwelling as *the* plight? Yet as soon as man *gives thought* to his homelessness, it is a misery no longer.'[17] Of course, the need for a physical home is a real plight, whatever Heidegger said, no doubt from the warmth of his own home, but the point is an important one. As others have said, a physical house does not in itself make a home or dwelling.

One of the things that characterises human beings is 'a staying *with* things', a belonging to what Heidegger called the 'fourfold' – earth, sky, divinities, mortals. Even when mortals turn 'inwards', taking stock of themselves, we do not leave behind our belonging to this fourfold. 'When, as we say, we come to our senses and reflect on ourselves, we come back to ourselves from things *without ever abandoning* our stay among things.'[18]

This tradition of thought has informed the work of the Philadelphia Association since the 1960s, both in its particular conception of therapeutic communities – houses to which people in emotional difficulty or distress can have recourse – and in its thinking about the practice of therapy in general. 'Suppose', wrote R. D. Laing, one of the founders of the Association, in an early brochure, 'one is looking for refuge from all the advice and treatment proposed or imposed by our well-intentioned parents, teachers, doctors, rulers and revolutionaries, who all think they know what is best for us? Then one wants an Asylum, a safe place, a haven, a sanctuary, a shelter; there one can have, if one wants, a pleasant room of one's own while other people see to it that there is food, warmth and shelter and try to hold the balance between care, concern, attention, mindfulness and letting be.'[19]

More recently, Robin Cooper has taken up this theme, describing the PA house as:

A household, where people may unpack, and live, and get on with it, with one another, as they wish. A place of co-habitation, where lives have implications for one another, where personal stories become woven together in the fabric, the 'nitty-gritty', the textures of everyday matters. A place where what matters shows. A house which honours the venerable tradition of hospitality to the stranger. A place where paperwork, in the forms of psychiatric records and clinical assessments, becomes irrelevant.[20]

While Robin Cooper is writing specifically about the thera-peutic community, at least as envisaged and run by the Philadelphia Association, what he says is directly relevant also to the practice of therapy in general. In individual psychotherapy too, if we follow this line of thought, there is a time and a place to unpack, metaphorically, a hospitality, in the sense of respect, patience, acceptance and an invitation to make oneself at home. Just as much as a therapeutic community, therapy is one of those places, in Bachelard's beautiful phrase, 'which invite us to come out of ourselves'.[21] All this, of course, is a challenge. It is not something that can be forced, but has to be created in a joint endeavour involving therapist and patient. And it is not easy. To paraphrase Mandelstam slightly, making a place for people to sit and talk takes as much trouble as scaling an Alp.[22]

In individual therapy too we encounter those 'strangers . . . who have lost their way, in one way or another. Those who have become disarticulated from human belonging, in one way or another. Those who would like to come in out of the cold.'[23] Here we meet those who do not feel at home in the world, who do not feel at home with others or even with themselves.

The place of therapy is a place of recollection, a place to dream. Just as much as the therapeutic community described by Robin Cooper, it is a place to dwell, to linger and to wander, as Robin Cooper notes, through the practice of free association. It is a place, an endeavour which calls not for calculative but meditative thinking. Here too, learning to dwell is not about the acquisition of new skills but about *recollection*. It involves a lingering, a taking of one's time.[24] Recollection in this context means not just or even primarily recollecting in the ordinary use of the term of remembering, but a gathering or bringing together again of what had been disparate and lost.

The place of therapy is a refuge, a shelter, 'a still point in a turning world',[25] a place of recollection, 'a coming to oneself, a retreat home with oneself as in a land of refuge, which answers to a hospitality, an expectancy, a human welcome.'[26] This hospitality or welcome to the other is based on an invitation by the therapist, an invitation to the patient to make herself at home, to stay awhile. It is a hospitality far more meaningful than that of the everyday with its social conventions. It involves a letting be, that is an allowing the patient. This is not an abandonment, a disregard for the patient's well-being. To the contrary, it is born precisely out of respect for that person. Paradoxically, perhaps, it also involves an engagement, of probing, encouragement, questioning, enabling as appropriate. Yet the word letting can also mean a hindering and this too we see in therapy, perhaps, in that we leave be and yet we also hinder in simultaneously refusing to leave be, in challenging and confrontation.

The 'therapeutic hour' is outside of normal time, the time of appointments and deadlines, free of interruptions and normal disturbances. True, it is itself an appointment and strictly bounded, with a beginning and an end, fixed by agreement beforehand, but within this allotted time, indeed because of it, the nature of time itself may change, may be heavy or light, may pass slowly or as in a moment. Above all, perhaps, the therapeutic hour has no agenda. Time here is truly free time, free of predetermined purpose, expectation and demand.

This space is, of course, under serious threat from a culture that is increasingly preoccupied with problems and their solutions, with time limits, results and outcomes. It is a space too that is often under threat of intrusion from third parties, usually well-meaning, parents, members of the 'caring professions', health service personnel and so on, those seeking reports of one kind or another. Here too as elsewhere we are in real danger of losing the conditions which make lingering, taking one's time, engaging in something that is non-purposive, if not impossible, very difficult indeed.

Like any host we extend an invitation, an invitation to make oneself at home. We cannot *make* someone feel at home but we can do what we can to facilitate this (to employ an overused word), to provide the conditions in which such a homemaking might become possible – a comfortable room, as peaceful as may be possible in a noisy world. In this regard, the therapeutic space, what we sometimes call the setting, is in itself an important and intrinsic part of our invitation, of our hospitality. Just as much as our personal manner of greeting and receiving people, it is an important communication to the patient, as Charles Rycroft has remarked:

> This setting includes, among other things, a quiet room with a couch in it, a closed door, regular and frequent appointments – and the analyst himself. This setting is itself a communication to the patient, since its details are all signs that the analyst is preparing to take up a certain attitude towards him, that he intends to listen to him, to concern himself with him without requiring him to be concerned with the analyst, and to protect the contact between them from external distraction.[27]

It would be ludicrous to try to specify the components of a comfortable room. A room, like the clothes we stand up in, speaks of *us*, of our tastes and inclinations, and is a personal matter. A room that makes us feel at home will, one hopes, work for others too. If I, as a therapist, do not feel at home in a room, it seems unlikely that anyone else will. If, on the other hand, I do feel at home there, there is at least a chance that others may come to do so too. So it does matter what a room looks like and feels like, which is why so many institutional rooms – anonymous and impersonal and, let's face it, often dingy or tasteless – seem to me so antithetical to the practice of good therapy. Anyone who has seen and been moved by the wondrous interiors of Braque or Matisse or Cézanne will know that a room – of whatever kind – is more than a collection of objects, but a coming together of those material things in a very particular, emotionally redolent way.

'A dwelling in the evening air': the place of therapy

The place of therapy is a place for thought, on the part of both parties present, a place for reflection, a place for recollection. But this can make it sound too lofty, too precious. It should also become a space of play or rather, for that makes it sound too purposive, a place where play is possible. It was Winnicott, of course, who thought about this more than anyone else and described it in his own inimitable way. 'Psychotherapy takes place', he wrote, 'in the overlap of two areas of playing, that of the patient and that of the therapist. Psychotherapy has to do with two people playing. The corollary of this is that where playing is not possible then the work done by the therapist is directed towards bringing the patient from a state of not being able to play into a state of being able to play.'[28] And later he adds: 'If the therapist cannot play, then he is not suitable for work.'[29]

This, as Zbigniew Kotowicz comments, is a long way from traditional psychoanalytic thinking, 'as radical a reversal of Freud's or Klein's determinism as one could imagine'. Play is not governed by the laws of determinism, it is not teleological, it has no pre-determined purpose, and while the concept of playing looks simple this is deceptive.[30]

The ability to play is not just about the capacity to be humorous or light-hearted, although these are important and are as much part of the therapeutic endeavour as the capacity for other feelings. It is about a capacity for creativity, a capacity which allows for things to emerge. It is in this respect closely connected to the ability to dream. This brings us inevitably to the writings of Gaston Bachelard who invented what he called topoanalysis – 'the systematic psychological study of the sites of our intimate lives'[31] – and who more than anyone else probed and elaborated upon the meanings of space for individuals. For Bachelard, dwelling is inseparable from the ability to dream. For him, the house is a place in which day-dreaming is possible:

113

The house we were born in is more than the embodiment of home, it is also an embodiment of dreams ... The house, the bedroom, the garret in which we were alone, furnished the framework for an interminable dream ... there exists for each one of us an oneiric house, a house of dream-memory, that is lost in the shadow of a beyond of a real past.[32]

The chief benefit of the house, Bachelard writes, is that it shelters day-dreaming, it protects the dreamer, it allows one to dream in peace:

... the house is one of the greatest powers of integration for the thoughts, memories and dreams of mankind ... Without it, man would be a dispersed being. It maintains him through the storms of the heavens and through those of life. It is body and soul. It is the human being's first world. Before he is 'cast into the world', as claimed by certain hasty metaphysicians, man is laid in the cradle of the house.[33]

Come what may, the house helps us to say, 'I will be an inhabitant of the world, in spite of the world.'[34] The therapist, of course, is not seeking to recreate home. In any case, for most people seeking therapy home may have been far from sweet, as Heller remarks in the passage quoted earlier. But are we not in our attitude of acceptance and interest providing that thing so dreaded by so many psychotherapists, a 'corrective emotional experience'? True, this is not our aim, it is not something we set out to do. True too that the patient is not a child and the therapist is not a mother or father, but if therapy is to have any value surely it must have an element of this? How can it not do? We listen, we respect, we attend. If appropriate we try to understand. All of this may have been lacking from the patient's past. 'You can't go home again,' realises the main character of Thomas Wolfe's novel

of the same name, but George Webber comes to accept this
as he understands that 'his dark roots' must now 'spread
outward – away from the hidden, secret, unfathomed past
that holds man's spirit prisoner – outward, outward towards
the rich and life-giving soil of a new freedom in the wide
world of all humanity'.[35] One cannot go home again but one
can still come to feel more at home. What is involved is not a
return to a home that one has known or imagined one has
known, but a finding of a new home, a new beginning, 'to
arrive where we started and know the place for the first
time'.[36] Coming home, being at home, furnishes one with a
sense of possibility, of a future, a place to go out from. And
here, as Robin Cooper notes in the context of therapeutic
communities, there is a paradox; 'one only leaves when one
arrives'.[37] One leaves when one feels at home, that one *can*
leave, leave as distinct from escape or run away or take flight.
Therapy is a lesson in learning to leave. I am often struck by
people's surprise when I remark that it is much easier to leave
a home where one has been happy than to leave one that is
unhappy. The latter forces or at least pushes one out; the
former allows one to leave, makes one's leaving possible, and
that is a great gift indeed.

Thom Gunn's poem 'A sketch of the great dejection' seems
to me particularly relevant here. It describes 'a place of
poverty, of inner and outer famine' where all movement has
stopped except that of the wind 'which is like a punishment
to face and hands'. We are here on 'marches of privation'
where the 'uneven lands' are without definition as the poet is
without 'potent words'. The narrator wonders how he can
possibly continue, thinking

> My body insisted on restlessness
>   having been promised love
> as my mind insisted on words
>   having been promised the imagination

115

but he goes on and the poem ends,

> and, though the landscape did not change,
> it came to seem after a while like a place of recuperation.

The landscape does not change but its feeling, its atmosphere, becomes something quite different. So too with therapy, the landscape – the place of therapy – does not change but it too may come to feel like a place of recuperation.[38]

So too in Wim Wenders' great film *Wings of Desire* there's a marvellous scene where the actor Peter Falk, playing himself, is standing sketching at a coffee and burger stall on a Berlin wasteground when he senses the presence of the angel Damiel who is, as angels are, invisible. The angel, it should be said, is increasingly contemplating giving up eternity for life on earth, for time and mortality. Falk says to the angel Damiel: 'I can't see you, but I know you're there . . . I wish I could see your face and look into your eyes and tell you how good it is to be here,' and he goes on to extol the pleasures of being human: 'To smoke, to have coffee and if you do it together it's fantastic. Or to draw. You take a pencil and you make a dark line, then you make a light line and together it's a good line. Or when your hands are cold, you rub them together. See, that's good, that feels good. There are so many good things. But you're not here.' And, to the bemusement of the stall keeper who wonders who on earth this guy is talking to, he extends his hand in a gesture of welcome.

In therapy I am not trying to persuade people to come into the world – they are already in it although sometimes only just – but I am, in a sense, holding out a hand of invitation, of hospitality, of possibility. And just as in Wenders' film the angel Damiel wishes to become a mortal because he has fallen in love with a trapeze artist, so for many people that we see the reawakening of sexual desire is both a sign of change and a condition for it.

116

'A dwelling in the evening air': the place of therapy

In the space of therapy we explore also the metaphorical places that people take up in the world, the positions that they occupy – dominant or submissive, generous or mean, withdrawn or outgoing, open or closed, doing or done to – the places that people know or think they know as 'theirs', as in the common notion of knowing one's place or being put in one's place. Position, as Levinas reminds us, is not something added on to human consciousness, rather consciousness comes out of a position. 'It is out of position, out of an immobility, that consciousness comes to itself.'[39] It is through taking up a position that the subject is affirmed.[40] Consciousness, in other words, is postural and is inextricably linked to the place that one occupies and takes up. Through therapy people may come, more consciously, more actively, to take up a place, to inhabit a place, rather than be defined and know their place. Therapy, like Bachelard's house, may help one to say, I will be an inhabitant of the world, in spite of the world.

In that 'intensest rendezvous', writes Wallace Stevens, 'We make a dwelling in the evening air,/in which being there together is enough.'[41] In therapy too we make a dwelling and in the process of this making other things may take their place.

6

'Speech for that unspoken': the poetics of therapy

The province of the poem is the world.

William Carlos Williams[1]

People who look for symbolic meanings fail to grasp the inherent poetry and mystery of the image. No doubt they sense this mystery, but they wish to get rid of it. They are afraid. By asking 'What does this mean?', they express a wish that everything be understandable. But if one does not reject the mystery, one has quite a different response. One asks other things.

René Magritte[2]

But poetry extends well beyond psychoanalysis on every side.

Gaston Bachelard[3]

What does poetry have to do with psychotherapy? The answer for most therapists granting any connection would be, I suspect, that poetic metaphor or poetic language in general can be useful or appropriate in the therapeutic encounter and that poetry (and literature in general) offers a huge resource that therapists or patients can call on as appropriate to put

118

what they are thinking and feeling into words. This is certainly true. As Murray Cox and Alice Theilgaard show in their excellent *Mutative Metaphors in Psychotherapy*,[4] psychotherapists would be foolish indeed to ignore the rich resource of poetic imagery and, in particular, the power of metaphor to touch the depths before the surface has stirred, in Bachelard's fine formulation of which their book may be seen as an extended elaboration. They also show how people who are not poets frequently in therapy come up with their own poetic language which expresses what they are after, often to considerable effect.

Others might point out that poets, along with other literary writers including playwrights and novelists, have insights into the human condition, an ability to see character in the most perceptive of ways and to describe what they see in ways that make us, their readers, see too. Indeed there is a whole tradition of psychotherapists from Freud onwards proffering psychoanalytic readings – often, in truth, misreadings – of literary works, from classical Greek drama to contemporary fiction, pressed into service to support some aspect of psychoanalytic theory.

But the relevance of poetry to therapy is something more fundamental than a shared interest in imagery or language. It is rather that poetics, deriving from the Greek *poesis*, is the art of creation and poetry is about creation, creation in language. It has no other medium. So too, I have argued, is psychotherapy about creation. It is a 'practical-poetic' activity, in the words of the psychoanalyst and social theorist Cornelius Castoriadis, whose outcome is, or ought to be, the self-alteration of the patient, a new being in a sense, at least a being who has a different attitude towards his drives, impulses and desires. So too is therapy about creating something through the medium of language. Therapy too has no other medium. Poetry is concerned with giving expression to the ineffable, the evanescent, just as therapy is. Given this

119

correspondence it is not perhaps surprising that the more I think about this, the more I practise the craft of psychotherapy, the more I come to believe that we have a great deal to learn not just from poets – many psychotherapists would accept this – but from those who have reflected upon and written about the *process* of writing poetry. I am thinking in particular of Wallace Stevens, Charles Simic and the Nobel Laureate, Seamus Heaney. In terms of a truly ethical poet, I am thinking of Paul Celan.[5]

THE LANGUAGE OF THE TRIBE

> *Our concern was speech and speech impelled us*
> *to purify the dialect of the tribe.*
>   T. S. Eliot (quoting Mallarmé)[6]

Poetry, the eighteenth-century philosopher Vico said, is the primary activity of the human mind. 'Man, before he arrives at the stage of forming universals, forms imaginary ideas . . . before he can articulate, he sings: before speaking in prose, he speaks in verse; before using technical terms he uses metaphors, and the metaphorical use of words is as natural to him as that which we call "natural".'[7] The making of poetry, in other words, is something like a second nature to human beings. Indeed we can see this in the number of people, from all sorts of walks of life and backgrounds, who feel moved, particularly relatively early in life, to write poetry of one sort or another.

There is, then, something quite ordinary about the making of poetry. This of course is not to say that making great or even just very good poetry is at all easy. It clearly isn't, but this ordinariness reminds us that the language of poetry need not be rarified or abstruse, removed from the language of the everyday. Far from it. It has rather to be, as Wallace Stevens puts it in his 'manifesto' poem, 'Of modern poetry':

> . . . living, to learn the speech of the place
> It has to face the men of the time and to meet
> The women of the time . . .[8]

The language of poetry, in other words, has to be the language of its context, of its place and time, and it may be utterly un-extraordinary, completely mundane (in the true sense of being *of the world*). It does not have to be unusual or ornate or in some way 'difficult'. But if it is to be any good, if it is to have any impact, the language of poetry does have to be free of cliché and unpredictable. As Stevens exhorts us elsewhere (in 'The man with the blue guitar'), we must not use 'the rotted names'.[9] It is what is done with language, however ordinary, that makes – or can make – for great poetry. When a man makes a poem, William Carlos Williams wrote, he takes words as he finds them and composes them 'into an intense expression of his perceptions and ardours that they may constitute a revelation in the speech that he uses'.[10]

In this context consider, for instance, what has been called the 'anti-poetry' of the Polish Tadeusz Różewicz who survived the destruction of his country in the Second World War, and whose work expressed his distrust of metaphor, of images, or beauty, and who sought to 'rehabilitate banality'. 'I cannot understand', Różewicz said in 1960, 'that poetry should survive when the men who created that poetry are dead. One of the premises and incentives for my poetry is a disgust with poetry.'[11] For Różewicz, the imagery of poetry was a detour, something that did not speed up but rather delayed the reader's encounter with the meaning of the work.[12] Consider too the poetry of Paul Celan, about whom I shall say more later. Celan could have turned his back on his mother tongue, German, as it was the language of the murderers – his own parents among the millions killed – and the destroyers. Instead Celan found himself refashioning the language, making it anew in order to press it into doing what he wanted of it, turning it back on itself.

There is a parallel here with some of those who seek psychotherapy, people for whom language has been anything but a thing of beauty but has always meant lying, deceit, dissimulation and so on. One of the earliest achievements of articulate speech, Bion once remarked, is how to make a fool of other people. It is one of the challenges facing the psychotherapist to reconstitute language in the service of truth.[13] (Therapy, too, it must be acknowledged, has created its own awful language. There is not only the dreadful pseudo-scientific technical language to which all therapeutic theoretical systems seem prey, but also the equally dreadful way in which ordinary language is colonised and degenerates into therapeutic cliché – we share, we hear, we are comfortable, thoughtful, sensitive, we hold, contain – all these and many more are words that it is now almost impossible to use, which have been lost to us through overuse).

Whatever form it takes, the language of poetry aims at precision, at getting the description, the feeling, the thought, as 'right' as possible. As Eliot puts it in 'Little Gidding':

> where every word is at home,
> Taking its place to support the others,
> The word neither diffident nor ostentatious,
> An easy commerce of the old and the new,
> The common word exact without vulgarity,
> The formal word precise but not pedantic,
> The complete consort dancing together[14]

And yet there is a paradox here. While poetic language is language at its most economic and precise, it is also at the same time language at its most free, its most allusive. Poetry is possibility, said Emily Dickinson, which means among other things, I believe, that poetry can bear a whole range of meanings and can be less constrained than prose. Poetry better than prose can bear ambiguity. 'Speak/But keep yes and no unsplit,' says Paul Celan in 'Speak, you also', 'He speaks truly who speaks the shade.'[15] Indeed we might say that such ambiguity is intrinsic to the poetic work. 'The machinations of ambiguity are among the very roots of poetry,' as William Empson puts it.[16] This is why, of course, the work of poetic interpretation is never-ending. Like the 'work' of psychotherapy it is never complete.

But because the poet must by definition work with language, so his work is inevitably open, if only potentially, to any who speak that language, however difficult it may at first seem. One does not have to 'understand' a poem (whatever that may mean) in order to appreciate it, in order to have one's own associations to it, in order to be moved by it. We need only get into it, open ourselves to it, immerse ourselves in it. Good criticism can help us here in suggesting what a poet may be getting at and how he is trying to do this. It also contextualises the poet, outlining his frame of reference. (Nor need one share the poet's general orientation in the world to be moved by the work which is why I, and many people I know, can love Eliot's poetry while loathing most of what he stood for, not least his contempt for the ordinary person and his anti-Semitism, which are communicated through his work. The vision of humanity that Eliot's poetry registers, Christopher Hampton rightly remarks, 'its attitude towards people . . . is at once negative, disdainful and reactionary'.[17]) Once a poem is published it becomes free of its author's intentions and becomes so to speak public property.

Hence Eliot's account of a religious journey in the *Four Quartets* gives way to many other kinds of reading. And so in psychotherapy, the psychotherapist does not have to understand what the patient or client is saying (again whatever that may mean) in order to appreciate it, be moved by it, associate to it, and to be with the patient in hearing, attending, making sense, making meaning.

The point of all this is not to suggest that psychotherapists have to be 'poetic' in an artificial sense of being clever or contrived in their language, or even of *seeking* to create something. (There is a salutary poem by Victor Hugo about a poet who welcomes a beggar into his home but is too caught up in the poetic resonances of his own gestures to listen to what the beggar is saying.) But we too aim at that balance of precision and freedom in language, at the recognition and acceptance of ambiguity, so that we too might create, or allow to happen, a 'revelation in speech'.

THE POETIC PROCESS

How does this putting into words come about, how is it done? Like the psychotherapist – or at least the kind of psychotherapist I am proposing one might be – the poet does not know beforehand what he wants to say. To think otherwise is a major misunderstanding. The writing of the poem, Charles Simic says, is not a search for the most effective way of 'gussying up' whatever ideas the poet may have had: 'If this were correct, poetry would simply repeat what has been thought and said before. There would be no poetic thinking in the way Heidegger conceives of it. There would be no hope that poetry would have any relation to truth.'[18] It is not the poet who speaks through the poem but the work itself – 'The poet is at the mercy of his metaphors.'[19] This of course is similar to what Merleau-Ponty and others I mentioned earlier

124

had to say about language, that it is not some kind of translation of previously existing thought but an accomplishment of such thought. The writer, Merleau-Ponty observed, does not control his thoughts from without but, rather, is himself 'a kind of new idiom, constructing itself, inventing ways of expression, and diversifying itself according to its own meaning'. And it is in poetry that this autonomy is most 'ostentatiously displayed'.[20]

This is not to suggest that poetic creation is a form of automatic writing such as that practised by the surrealists and others. It is not *just* a matter of letting something speak through one. Poetry requires craft and technique as well as inspiration. 'We put words on paper,' writes Alasdair Gray in lines that I have on the wall facing me as I write this, 'notice these are not very good, exciting or true, and the work begins.' For writing of any kind *is work*. It is in the balance of these, perhaps, more than anything that the art lies. To write well in any way you have to be able to use words, to love words and images, but you also have to be able to enjoy playing with language and images. And the more allusive the language you use, the better the poem you are likely to create.

This, of course, is also true of other modes of artistic creation. The creative act, as so many have testified, has much more to do with an *attitude, a position of waiting, and of allowing*, than with conscious striving. The German film-maker Wim Wenders, for instance, has written of the problems of knowing too much in advance about how a film may be, of how this can get in the way of making the film, and of the importance of allowing things to happen in the process of film-making. Describing as a 'violation' certain forms of film-making, where for instance the end is filmed first, Wenders has described how he would find himself during the filming of his *Kings of the Road*: 'At night, in some village hotel room, I would sometimes be overcome with terror. I would

125

be sitting around, and it would be midnight, or two or four in the morning, and I still had no idea what we'd be shooting in the morning.'[21]

The poet and the therapist both require an attitude of reverie, a capacity for waiting, for allowing, for not getting in the way of what might emerge. They both need that 'negative capability' that Keats spoke of. They require too an ability to dream – the psychoanalyst, Bachelard says, thinks too much and does not dream enough[22] – and to day-dream, for poetic activity of whatever kind, as the philosopher Jacques Maritain put it, is 'a margin of day-dreaming activity'. Yet it is a capacity, by no means confined to poets, which 'many have murdered in themselves'.[23] The psychotherapist, like the poet, seeks to free this capacity in himself and in doing so can help to free it in others, bring it back to life.

Few recent poets have been so preoccupied with the process of writing as W. S. Graham, who died in 1986. 'What a mysterious, unsubstantial business it is, writing poetry,' Graham wrote to a friend. 'After one finishes a poem which seems to work one says Ha Ha now I'll write another because I know how to do it but it is not so. There is the silence before one just as difficult to disturb significantly as before. What one has learned is inadequate against the new silence presented.'[24]

In his haunting poem, 'Malcolm Mooney's Land', Graham wrote of this struggle for speech, against the silence, as though it were analogous to a journey across bleak and frozen terrain:

> From wherever it is I urge these words
> To find their subtle vents, the northern dazzle
> Of silence cranes to watch.

His words 'crackle in the early air' and he asks that his 'impediment mean no ill/And be itself a way':

126

> And why is it there has to be
> Some place to find, however momentarily
> To speak from, some distance to listen to?

In the end, the poet seems to have found some sense of resolution, however temporary; it is words and language that have become the reality.

> I have made myself alone now.
> Outside the tent endless
> Drifting hummock crests.
> Words drifting on words.
> The real unabstract snow.[25]

Another poem, 'The Constructed Space', might well have been written about psychotherapy:

> . . . Anyhow here we are and never
> Before have we two faced each other who face
> Each other now across this abstract scene
> Stretching between us.[26]

We know what we are saying, Graham writes, 'Only when it is said and fixed and dead'. But even then doubt creeps in for perhaps we never know what we have said, 'what lonely meanings are read/Into the space we make'. And yet one must always make the attempt:

> I say this silence or, better, construct this space
> So that somehow something may move across
> The caught habits of language to you and me.[27]

Eliot too, by whom Graham was clearly influenced, addressed directly this struggle with language, albeit with his characteristic sense of futility:

Words strain
Crack and sometimes break, under the burden,
Under the tension, slip, slide, perish,
Decay with imprecision, will not stay in place,
Will not stay still.[28]

The 'intolerable wrestle with words and meanings'[29] can for
Eliot only end in a kind of failure:

. . . every attempt
Is a wholly new start, and a different kind of failure
Because one has only learnt to get the better of words
For the thing one no longer has to say, or the way in which
One is no longer disposed to say it. And so each venture
Is a new beginning, a raid on the inarticulate.[30]

The nature of the failure is, however, the crucial point. Some
failures are better – and worse – than others, as Beckett made
clear in his famous lines, 'No matter. Try again. Fail again.
Fail better.'

THE ETHICS OF POETRY

To give words to what has been without words is the task of
the poet. The poet seeks to render into language, into words,
that which, whatever, has so far evaded it. Poetry is a 'raid
on the inarticulate', in Eliot's fine phrase,[31] 'a rough translation from wordlessness into words' in Charles Simic's.[32] Simic
says:

My hunch has always been that our deepest experiences
are wordless. There may be images, but there are no words
to describe the gap between seeing and saying, for example.

The labor of poetry is finding ways through language to point to what cannot be put into words.[33]

It is not that the poet must write about something unusual, far from it. Although he may do this, much poetry, perhaps most, is concerned with experiences and events or thoughts and feelings which can be known to us, accessible to us, even if they are not familiar. Indeed, one might say that sometimes the poet's task is precisely to render unfamiliar that which is familiar, to make us see or look at things anew. I think here of Neruda's manifesto 'On impure poetry' in which he calls for

> poetry worn away as if by acid by the labour of hands, impregnated with sweat and smoke, smelling of lilies and urine, splashed by the variety of what we do, legally or illegally. A poetry as impure as old clothes, as a body, with its foodstains and its shame, wrinkles, observations, dreams, wakefulness, prophecies, declarations of love and hate, stupidities, shocks, idylls, political beliefs, negations, doubts, affirmations, taxes.[34]

I think here too of a poet like Edwin Morgan who can write of the deepest things – love, human solidarity, poverty, cruelty – but who can surprise and delight us too writing about the most simple things in life, like watching a decorator at work, eating an apple, hearing a girl sing a song, and so on. The poet's role, Wallace Stevens wrote, was 'to help people live their lives' and he did this, not just by creating what Stevens called 'the supreme fictions' which we need to live our lives, but, again, by giving words to the thoughts and feelings which 'are all the truth that we shall ever experience'.[35] It is by the poet's grace, wrote Bachelard, that 'we have become the pure and simple subject of the verb "to marvel".'[36]

Poetry aims too, as Seamus Heaney has articulated, at redress. Heaney uses the word 'redress' not just in its primary sense of reparation of, or satisfaction or compensation for, a wrong sustained, but notes also an obsolete meaning which seems to me relevant to what brings many people to seek therapy, 'to set (a person or a thing) upright again; to raise again to an erect position. Also *fig.* to set up again, restore, re-establish.' So in what does this 'redress' lie? For Heaney it comes from poetry being a 'glimpsed alternative, a revelation of potential that is denied or constantly threatened by circumstances', and he goes on to say that what Vaclav Havel has said about hope can be said about poetry too, that it is 'an orientation of the spirit, an orientation of the heart; it transcends the world that is immediately experienced'.[37] Poetry must not simplify, its projections and inventions 'have to be a match for the complex reality which surrounds it and out of which it is generated ... It becomes another truth to which we can have recourse, before which we can know ourselves in a more fully empowered way.'[38] Therapy too, of course, is about a glimpsed alternative, a revelation of the potential that is in everyone.

The redressive power of poetry comes also from its inevitably social nature. Every poet inevitably writes within a tradition, of what has been written before, whether he works with or against that tradition. It is not just that the poet has been influenced by people he has read but that poetry almost invariably leads us to other writers and other work through allusions, borrowings, homages and so on. Eliot is but the most extreme example of this with his cullings from and collage of everything from the Upanishads to Dante, from the Bible to the demotic. Poetry, in other words, is or can be an opening into a world and that world is the world of language.

Poetry also connects the reader with the wider world of which he is a part. This idea of the social nature of the poem may seem paradoxical for, although one may well hear a poem read in public, the reading of poetry is essentially a private act. As Joseph Brodsky says in his Nobel lecture, 'Uncommon visage', lots of things can be shared, even a lover, but not a poem, for 'a poem in particular addresses a man tête-a-tête, entering with him into direct – free of any go-betweens – relations'.[39] And yet the poet is a social creature. It is not just that he uses the language of his tribe and can do no other, but as Nadezhda Mandelstam wrote in *Hope Against Hope*:

> The work of the poet, as a vehicle for world harmony, has a social character – that is – it is concerned with the doings of the poet's fellow men, among whom he lives and whose fate he shares. He does not speak 'for them', but with them, nor does he set himself apart from them: otherwise he would not be a source of truth.[40]

The poet, in other words, is connected to the people among whom he finds himself, he is 'an intermediary between people and the world in which they live' (Stevens), and yet the poem is still or can be something intensely personal. It is, Seamus Heaney has said, a 'divination, a revelation of self to the self' just as much as 'restoration to the culture itself'.[41] For Charles Simic the poem is an attempt at self-recovery, self-recognition, self-remembering, 'the marvel of being again'. That this happens at times, happens in poems in many different and contradictory ways, is as great a mystery as the mystery of being itself and cause for serious thought.[42]

Never one to make modest claims for his calling, Wallace Stevens argued that poetry had taken the place of religion. 'After one has abandoned a belief in God,' he wrote, 'poetry is the essence which takes its place as life's redemption.'[43] One does not have to go as far as Stevens but he is saying something important about the place that poetry can have in the lives of individual men and women. It is something of a higher order to which we turn when we have had enough of the commonplace, the banal, the trivial, the meaningless, and want, indeed need, something meaningful. Poetry is, in other words, a deeply, indeed fundamentally, ethical activity. It is ethical in that it is a form of communication, from the poet to his readers and from the reader with himself. It is concerned with capturing, if only for an instant, and communicating, if only fleetingly, the things that matter in the lives of men and women. It is concerned, in the end, with truth, with looking behind the façades of the everyday. This does not mean that poetry has to be earnest – any more than therapy has to be earnest. Not at all. To quote Charles Simic again: 'It's not so much what the words mean that is crucial, but what they show and reveal. The literal leads to the figurative, and inside every poetic figure of value there's a theater where a play is in progress. The play is about gods and demons and the world in its baffling presence and variety.'[44]

Poetry is not some kind of luxury but something that we need. Springing as it does from the imagination, it is what marks us from the animals. 'Human life without some form of poetry,' Randall Jarrell wrote, 'is not human life but animal existence.'[45] When man organises rationally, writes Cornelius Castoriadis, about whom I shall have more to say in the next chapter, he does nothing but reproduce, repeat or prolong already existing forms. When he 'organises poetically', however, 'he gives form to the Chaos . . . to the Chaos of what is and that within man himself'. Art is not only a window on the Chaos, 'it abolishes our tranquil and stupid assurance about our daily life; it reminds us that we forever live at the edge of the Abyss – which is the main thing an autonomous being knows.'[46]

Poetry therefore helps us to live our lives. It tells us, it reminds us, that there is always something more than what we are seeing, that there is more to our experience, whether this be loving someone, looking out of a window, sitting in a café or whatever, than what is immediately apparent. And it is an attempt to put us in touch with that deeper, richer experience. In a sense, then, Stevens was right in his inflated claim about poetry replacing religion in that it serves as a constant reminder of the utter wonder of the world and of our place in it.

No poet this century, I believe, better warrants the epithet ethical than Paul Celan.[47] Born Paul Antschel in German-speaking Bukovina in 1920, the man who would become Paul Celan survived the depredations of forced German labour while, in an internment camp, his father died from typhus and his mother was shot in the back of the head. These experiences – and the responses of the world to them – marked the body of the poetry that Paul Celan was to write from the mid-1940s until his death by suicide in Paris in 1970 at the age of forty-nine. But the ethical dimension of this poetry does not reside in its subject matter alone, which is by no means confined to the 'disaster' although the poems are inescapably marked by it, but in its stance, its position in the world. Celan articulated this in a speech, 'The Meridian', when he was awarded the prestigious Georg Buchner Prize in 1960.[48] In this highly allusive and elliptical speech Celan addressed the relationship between poetry and individual existence, with the poem as a step on the way to both self and other: 'Expand art? No. But accompany art into your own unique place of no escape. And set yourself free.'

The poem, Celan said in his speech, attempts to pay careful attention to everything that it encounters; 'it has a finer sense of detail, of outline, of structure, of color, and also of the "movements" and the "suggestions".' But this sense of detail is not a matter of competing with other means of seeing. 'No, it is a concentration which remains aware of all our dates.' (Celan is here referring to history, both personal and political, and to those momentous events which always take place on a particular day.) The poem, he says, wants to reach the other,

133

'it needs this Other, it needs a *vis-à-vis*. It searches it out and addresses it. Each thing, each person is a form of the Other for the poem, as it makes for this Other.' The poem 'becomes dialogue' but it is often 'despairing dialogue'. It is only in the realm of this dialogue that that which is addressed 'take[s] form and gather[s] around the I who is addressing and naming it. But the one who has been addressed and who, by virtue of having been named, has, as it were, become a thou, also brings its otherness along into the present . . .'[49]

Later in his speech Celan speaks of poems as 'circuitous paths from thou to thou', paths on which language acquires a voice: 'these are encounters, a voice's paths to a perceiving thou, creaturely paths, sketches of existence perhaps, a sending oneself ahead to oneself, in the process of searching for oneself . . . a kind of homecoming.'[50]

Poetry, in other words, for Paul Celan was always a reaching out to the other, a search for this other, without, of course, any guarantee that such an encounter would arise. It was 'a message in a bottle', with all the desperation and haphazardness that that image conjures up. And it was only in this reaching out to the other that one encountered one's own self.

There are many echoes in Celan's 'The Meridian', it will be heard, of Levinas although there is no knowing whether the poet had even heard of Levinas either at the time of his speech or before his death ten years later. It is not surprising then to find Levinas addressing Celan in his short but dense text, 'Being and the other: on Paul Celan'.[51] Levinas begins his text with a remark Celan once made to an editor that he saw no difference between a poem and a handshake. (Levinas himself had written in *Existence and Existents*, begun while he too was a prisoner of the Germans, 'To shake hands with a friend is to express one's friendship for him, but it is to convey that friendship as something inexpressible, and indeed as something unfulfilled, a permanent desire.'[52]) For Celan, the poem existed at the moment 'of pure touch, of pure contact . . . a way of giving even to the hand that gives'. Through 'its for the other', Levinas said, Celan's poetry made possible 'the whole miracle of giving'. Do not poetry and art begin, Levinas asked, precisely in their 'for-other speaking to the other . . ., in signalling this very giving of the sign, in love speaking that love, in lyricism?' There is no doubt of Levinas's answer to this question or that the poet who most exemplified this stance was Celan. There is no one whose work more represented that 'finality without end' that was the hallmark of the poetic movement, 'as if in going toward the other I were reunited with myself in a soil that would be, henceforth, native', no one for whom the act of writing poetry more constituted 'the spiritual act *par excellence*'.

We have come full circle then. Poetry is ethical in the sense that Levinas gives to it and which I am using in that it is a reaching out to the other. It is an invitation, a welcome, a hospitality, the promise or at least the offer of a meeting, an offer without guarantee for either party.

Psychotherapy too, of course, is about giving words to the wordless, finding 'speech for that unspoken' in Eliot's beautiful phrase.[53] We hope to render speakable what has been unspeakable. This formulation is often used to refer to terrible trauma that the individual has experienced but it need not be limited to this. The unspeakable to the individual may well be something quite ordinary, the most ordinary feelings, for instance, if there has been an injunction on them. In therapy too we engage with people whose difficulty is not that they have too few words but too many, where these many are somehow insufficient or inadequate, where all the words in the world, or so it seems, somehow cannot speak the truth. Therapy too, as I have said, is about the recognition of a glimpsed alternative, a revelation of potential denied, an expression of a faith that words be found, words that are more honest and truthful.

135

Many people seeking psychotherapy are engaged in a despairing dialogue, sending out messages in bottles. In therapy as in poetry our aim – or one of them at least – is to put things into words, not *for* those we are seeing but *with* them, to assist them in finding their own voice, their own idiom, just as each poet seeks to find his own voice or idiom. Psychotherapy is a place where one can learn about language, about what words can do and be, and about speaking. And as with poetry our medium is, and can only be, language.

7

Psychotherapy in the world

Many are oppressed, many are in need;
and whoever thinks is threatened.

Otto Fenichel[1]

It is not what is, but what could be and should be,
that has need of us.

Cornelius Castoriadis[2]

Ethics, if it is to be meaningful, can never be limited to the one to one, face to face encounter. By extension it has to move from my relations as an individual with other individuals into my relations with the wider social context that I inhabit and which gives form to me. It has to move into and become politics. In the context that I am speaking of here the ethical stance that is embodied in psychotherapy requires us to engage also with the world in which psychotherapy takes its place.

An objective observer of the world of psychotherapy today would get little sense of the political radicalism that has been part of the history of psychotherapy at least since Freud's day. She would see, in general, a profession which is profoundly conservative (despite its liberal political leanings) and which is, moreover, almost by definition cut off and isolated from the external world outside the consulting room. The clinicians attend to the individual, forgetting that the very concept of that individual is formed in a social context. This observer would also see a world in which academic psychoanalysis flourishes, often under the tutelage of people who would align themselves with the political left, and yet remains firmly bound within the walls of academe.

In a sense, psychotherapy has fitted in well with our individualistic times. It provides a way of being individual, of attending to the individual, while avoiding the materialism and ruthlessness which have been hallmarks of individualism at large. No one perhaps has made this critique more forcibly than the Jungian James Hillman who goes so far as to argue that psychotherapy has contributed directly to a withdrawal from politics and to a decline in the actual world. In his provocative book of conversations with journalist Michael Ventura, *We've Had a Hundred Years of Psychotherapy and the World's Getting Worse*, Hillman argues:

There is a decline in political sense. No sensitivity to the real issues. Why are the intelligent people – at least among the white middle class – so passive now? Why? Because the sensitive, intelligent people are in therapy! They've been in therapy in the United States for thirty, forty years, and during that time there's been a tremendous political decline in this country ... Every time we try to deal with our outrage over the freeway, our misery over the office and the lighting and the crappy furniture, the crime on the street, whatever – every time we try to deal with that by going to therapy with our rage and fear, we're depriving the political world of something. And therapy, in its crazy way, by emphasising the inner soul and ignoring the outer soul, supports the decline of the actual world. Yet therapy goes on blindly believing that it's curing the outer world by making better people. We've had that for years and years and years: 'If everybody went into therapy we'd have better buildings, we'd have better people, we'd have more consciousness.' It's not the case.[3]

Elsewhere Hillman has criticised psychotherapy for its dedication to individualism, itself a legacy of the Freudian concept of the person which is for him 'a sociological or ecological reflection of a particular psychological climate which also saw the apogee of colonialism, industrialism, capitalism etc.'[4]

Hillman has to be taken seriously, not just because of his standing as a pre-eminent therapist and thinker himself, but because he is on to something, although in the end he goes too far, I believe. While it is true that psychotherapy has not contributed to meaningful political activity on any significant scale, to blame it for political decline seems to me wide of the mark. The turn to psychotherapy by many radicals, leftists and feminists was not a *cause* of political decline but rather a *sign* of political defeat, the defeat, however temporary it may turn out to be, of the project of socialism.

It is possible to consider the engagement of psychotherapy and the world at three levels. First, there is the application of psychotherapy to the world, for instance the attempt to understand social and political processes through psychoanalytic concepts such as splitting, projection, resistance and so on. Second, there is the question of the politics of the world of psychotherapy, including questions of training, professional regulation, provision of service and so on. Third, there is the politics of psychotherapeutic practice as such. I want to look at each of these areas in turn.

PSYCHOTHERAPY AND THE WORLD

During the 1970s and 1980s, considerable numbers of feminists, leftists and other radicals turned to psychotherapy both as personal therapy and as a theoretical tool for understanding social processes, particularly mechanisms of domination and factors obstructing social and political change. Such people frequently drew inspiration from the Freudo-Marxist tradition of Wilhelm Reich, Otto Fenichel and Herbert Marcuse, as well as more recent writers such as Russell Jacoby and Joel Kovel. Others looked to the ideas of Lacan and his followers, while others have looked to develop the work of Klein and Bion.

Such endeavours have clearly yielded a great deal of academic knowledge – as shown in a wide range of books, journals, conferences, seminars, academic courses, research centres and projects – and psychoanalysis in particular has, arguably, taken a hold within the general culture as never before. But what has this produced in terms of political *practice*? Very little would be the short answer. Those who began by hoping to bring the personal and the political closer together ended up by abandoning politics altogether and finding consolation in the self-contained politics of psychoanalytic theory and practice.

Academic psychoanalysis has produced a rather self-referential group of textual experts, talking to one another in an exclusive and rarified language about their own and others' texts. In this respect, it has become part of that process, described by Russell Jacoby in his book, *The Last Intellectuals*, of a retreat by intellectuals from an active engagement in public and political life into the academy. The public intellectuals of before, people like Edmund Wilson, Dwight Macdonald and Lewis Mumford, sought and wrote, Jacoby argues, for a wide public; their present-day counterparts write for each other.[5] While one could name dozens of people regarded as expert in their own field of psychoanalysis or cultural, feminist or literary studies, one could name hardly anyone in the field of psychoanalysis who could in any way be regarded as a public intellectual, that is someone who seeks a mass audience outside of the academic world. The 'turn to psychotherapy' taken by many leftists, feminists and other radicals in the 1970s and 1980s has ended up as a retreat from collective engagement and a search for individual consolation in the self-contained politics of psychoanalytic theory in the academy.

When the world has become a text, as it seems to have become for our cultural commentators, there is nothing really to do, except to interpret and comment. Some such commentary and interpretation may be and has been interesting, but it should not be mistaken for politics, that is for questioning, challenging and ultimately trying to change relations of power, inequality and injustice. At worst, we have, as people as different politically as George Steiner and Cornelius Castoriadis have remarked, a culture of secondariness, a culture of commentary which is not at all concerned with thinking or trying to think new things, but rather with commenting. Even then the commentary is not even restricted to original work but commenting on the commentary. Hence the absurd rise to prominence in recent years of the 'critic', as opposed to the original creative writer or thinker, whether on late night television discussion programmes, in the books pages of newspapers and magazines, or in the culture at large. For such people, as Aijaz Ahmad remarks in his marvellous book, *In Theory* – a much-needed corrective to the excesses of postmodernism, post-structuralism and especially 'literary theory' – 'Any attempt to *know* the world as a whole, or to hold that it is open to rational comprehension, let alone the desire to change it, [is] to be dismissed as a contemptible attempt to construct "grant narratives" and "totalizing (totalitarian) knowledges".'[6]

But what then of those attempts to 'know the world', to engage with it at the political level? Does psychoanalysis actually have anything to say about political events that can contribute to a practical and political response, a response that enables people who want to change things to intervene more effectively? To go back to the founder of our discipline, as we seem always to find ourselves doing, Freud clearly thought that psychoanalysis did have something to say that was relevant to an understanding of society and social processes. In his 1913 article, 'Claims of psychoanalysis to the interest of non-psychological sciences', Freud spoke of the capacity of psychoanalysis 'to throw light on the origins of our great cultural institutions'. But it is interesting to note that while addressing himself to philosophy, psychology and even sociology, Freud did not think it worthwhile to address himself to the subject of politics. In any case, writing a political character reference for psychoanalysis, as David Ingleby has put it, is no straightforward matter.[7] Freud's own political views were ambiguous and his political and social writings, for example *Civilisation and Its Discontents*, *Totem and Taboo* and more immediate and topical writings such as 'Why war?', are frequently highly speculative. Anthropologically, such works are marked by a profound ignorance and what we might now regard as a deep Eurocentrism. And, of course, Freud merely ended up substituting myths, for instance of the primal horde, when he could offer no final explanation, which he felt he had to do and which, of course, was impossible. Psychologically, much of this work is guilty of the kind of reductionism that we would now deplore. This is not confined to Freud but marks much of the writing that has followed.

Politics certainly needs to recognise, as Michael Rustin has argued, the importance of the emotional in the life of the human subject if it is not to have a limited and flawed conception of human beings, and here psychotherapy has an important contribution to make.[8] But too often psychoanalytic approaches to politics have been reductionist. The problem stems, as Andrew Samuels has written, from approaching a whole culture or large chunks of it 'as if it were an

individual or even as if it were a baby'.[9] In this infantilisation
of culture, a version of personality development, couched in
judgemental terms, is used to understand a collective and
cultural process:

> If we look in this manner for pathology in the culture, we
> will surely find it. If we are looking with a particular
> psychological theory in mind, then, lo and behold, the
> theory will explain the pathology. But this is a retrospective
> prophecy (to use a phrase of Freud's), twenty-twenty hind-
> sight . . . If we are interested in envy and greed, then we
> will find envy and greed in capitalistic organisation. If we
> set out to demonstrate the presence of archetypal patterns,
> such as projection of the shadow, in the geopolitical rela-
> tions of the superpowers, then, without a doubt, they will
> seem to leap out at us. But so often this is just more of the
> maddening rectitude of the analyst who has forgotten that
> we influence what we analyse.[10]

So when psychoanalysis has been brought to bear on
political issues, the results have been often banal and at worst
deeply normative and conformist. On the subject of racism,
to take one of the most horrendous and destructive phenomena of our century and earlier ones, the world of psychoanalysis has had remarkably little to say. (This, paradoxically,
may be a blessing, given the banality of most of what has
been said.) In most such writing, racism is reduced to a
universal facet of individual psychic life, a matter of projective
mechanisms, albeit writ large on the world stage. History,
anthropology, sociology and political economy go out the
window, that is if they were ever even admitted in the first
place.[11]

On the question of sexuality the record of psychoanalysis
is, if anything, even worse. As Noreen O'Connor and Joanna
Ryan have so cogently shown, psychoanalysis has, with few

exceptions, consistently asserted that male and female homosexuality are perversions from some supposedly normal
course of sexual development, and has done so on the basis
of precious little evidence and very much more in the way of
circular argument and self-fulfilling logic.[12]

On other issues, the picture is scarcely better. Much was
made at the time a few years ago when many British psychoanalysts entered the political arena through the formation of
Psychoanalysts Against Nuclear War. There can be no doubt
of the good intentions of those involved but what is striking
is the fact that it was this issue that so prompted analysts to
depart from their traditional political disinterestedness, as
though there had been no major questions before. As for
what was said on the subject, once again we were witness to
a reduction of major political developments to 'regression
from the depressive position and the mobilization of para-
noid/schizoid mechanisms, splitting and projection . . . infan-
tile omnipotence and the death instinct and destructive
psychotic defences', to quote from Hanna Segal's summary of
her much-cited article, 'Silence is the real crime'.[13]

So too at the time of the build-up to the Gulf War in 1991,
many psychotherapists and psychoanalysts attended a meeting convened at the Institute of Psycho-Analysis at which a
statement of protest was agreed. Once again it is not difficult
to appreciate what brought those people together. But what
this statement had to say was hardly of major import. Did it
really assist our understanding of what was happening or our
ability to influence developments to be told that there was a
lot of projection going on on the stage of world politics?

The constructive fusion of psychoanalysis and politics that
so many hoped for and worked for has not failed to materi-
alise because of the limitations of those involved. Many of
them are, after all, capable people. Rather, it may be that the
endeavour is doomed from the start, that, as Cornelius Castoriadis said in an interview a few years ago, the further

psychoanalysis moves from the individual in the framework of a session, the more questionable its observations become.[14]

Does this mean that psychoanalysis can contribute nothing to politics? No. Is there nothing in the realm of politics to concern psychotherapists? Far from it. But what can be done is limited and we have to be a little more modest in our claims for this discipline. It can help identify cultural trends as Christopher Lasch did in his seminal work *The Culture of Narcissism*.[15] It can also contribute to an understanding of how societies bring about the character types which are their 'concrete bearers', as Castodiadis puts it, and how this might be changed.[16] Psychoanalysis certainly has many things to tell us about unconscious processes at the individual level, and the thinking of Bion and others in the group relations tradition can yield valuable insights into the difficulties that people seem so often to face when they come together to do something politically. Moving beyond this, however, we must tread warily.

Let us note here too that the politics of psychotherapy can also be of a deeply conservative and reactionary nature. It is far from uncommon to hear one-time radicals or even revolutionaries who have been in psychoanalysis or psychotherapy disavow their political pasts on the basis of some supposed psychopathology of which they are now free or at least aware. So too is it not uncommon to encounter psychotherapeutic discussions of political or social issues which are also pathologising. I am thinking here not just of a book such as *Freud or Reich?* by the orthodox psychoanalysts Janine Chasseguet-Smirgel and Bela Grunberger which dismisses any idea of social change as illusion and likens political ideology to the fantasy of schizophrenics.[17] Here, for instance, is a more recent remark from a respected psychoanalytic organisational consultant writing about the changing world of work: 'The long-running national soap opera of the 1984-5 miners' strike provided wonderful support for our schizoid defences: either

145

Scargill or Thatcher could be chosen as the hero to identify with or the villain to be denigrated, and the country divided among them.'[18] And, let it be noted, this statement is not one that is taken up in any way by the book's editors in their discussion of his contribution. A great deal could be said about these few lines but let me limit myself to two observations. One, here is one of the most important industrial struggles and social conflicts of the post-war period, if not the century, reduced to a 'soap opera'. Two, if anyone is guilty of simplification it is the writer, to whom it does not seem to occur that many people – myself included – supported the cause of the miners, not because we saw Scargill as 'hero' (far from it) or Thatcher as 'villain', but because we believed the miners had justice on their side and the conflict was about something much more than the fate of one industry and the future of one particular section of society. It inevitably raised questions about the whole notion of community and the social organisation of the economy. The remark also implies that those who supported the government (or even those who supported the government) did so unthinkingly and uncritically.

THE POLITICS OF PRACTICE

Any discussion of the politics of psychotherapy must also attend to the politics of psychotherapeutic practice. We need to be clear about what we think we are doing with those people that we see. This too is a political matter. To ask an old-fashioned but still relevant question: are we merely acting as Band-aids for the fall-out of a sick and disabling society, at least for those able to pay, or are we doing something else? Psychotherapy is, as I have argued, an ethical undertaking whose aim is, dare I say it, the relief of mental suffering and distress. But it is political too in that psychic distress cannot

146

be divorced from the social and material context in which it occurs, any more than can our responses, including our preconceived ideas about the nature of the human subject.

In the 1970s, there were various attempts to create what its practitioners called 'radical therapy', that is psychotherapy explicitly aimed at political change. Yet, as Russell Jacoby commented, 'even the most extended therapy remains therapy . . . there is no such activity as radical therapy.'[19] Nearly a decade later, Jacoby was writing that a radical emancipatory therapy remained a 'hopeless hope'. Where, he asked, was the evidence?

> The project is tantalising, yet more convincing on the conceptual than on the concrete level. It seems possible and desirable to correlate the individual emancipation of therapy with the social emancipation of politcal practice, but the imperatives of politics may diverge from the imperatives of therapy. Loyalty to the individual must respect the specific patterns of unhappiness; to link them aggressively, even unaggressively, to the social evil seconds the injuries.[20]

I take Jacoby's point. At the same time, there have been in recent history significant attempts at what one might call 'political therapy' which deserve to be remembered and which can be learned from even if they cannot be directly emulated. I have in mind the work of the young, revolutionary psychiatrist Frantz Fanon, and his treatment of guerrillas and others during the war of Algerian independence and his analysis of the psychological disorders induced by colonial war described in *The Wretched of the Earth*.[21] So too I have in mind the work of the Austrian-born psychoanalyst, Marie Langer, who in the 1970s left the official psychoanalytic organisation in Argentina in opposition to its supposed neutrality and apoliticism in the years of military repression, and who worked with political refugees in Mexico. Later she would work with those caught up in the Nicaraguan civil war where she promoted what she called 'psychoanalysis without the couch', which involved among other things teaching ten basic psychoanalytic ideas to be applied in different forms of therapy.[22] In South Africa, there was the work of the Sanctuary Counselling Team, providing therapy to people involved in, and affected by, the struggle against the apartheid regime.[23] We, of course, in Britain in the 1990s do not find ourselves in these situations. Britain is not anti-imperialist Algeria or Nicaragua or apartheid South Africa, but these experiences are there to be drawn upon and their legacy can be traced to the psychotherapeutic work, largely unsung, that is undertaken for example with refugees and asylum-seekers, with people who have undergone torture, as well as in community-based therapy and counselling projects.

More generally, the correlation of therapy and politics can also be attempted in another way, albeit in a form different to that envisaged by the proponents of radical or political therapy. This lies in the attempt to link what as therapists we see in the clinical encounter with the organisation of society as whole. How, *precisely and specifically*, are individual lives emotionally damaged by the existing order of things? That seems to me the question or at least one of the questions. What are the social causes, or at least the conditions that give rise to depression, anxiety, lack of self-worth, impotence? Here there is already a history, a tradition from which to learn and on which to build. It is the history of the 'political Freudians', that remarkable second and third generation of psychoanalysts so beautifully evoked by Russell Jacoby in his book, *The Repression of Psychoanalysis: Otto Fenichel and the political Freudians*.[24] 'Neuroses are social diseases,' wrote Fenichel, at the end even of his most seemingly orthodox work, *The Psychoanalytic Theory of Neurosis*. Fenichel struggled all the time against the biological and cultural reductions of orthodox psychoanalysis – he criticised the

148

British analysts for 'an exaggeration of biology' – they were 'the consequences of experience' and experience was social. Neuroses, he insisted, corresponded to a given and historically developed social milieu and could not be changed 'without corresponding change in the milieu'.[25]

Similarly Erich Fromm, who castigated psychoanalysis and psychoanalysts for a retreat into 'conformism and the search for respectability' after the First World War, called for a 'creative renewal of psychoanalysis ... possible only if it overcomes its positivistic conformism and becomes again a radical and challenging theory in the spirit of radical humanism.' Specifically, Fromm said, psychoanalysis had to address the psychological phenomena constituting the pathology of contemporary society – alienation, anxiety, loneliness, the fear of feeling deeply, lack of activeness [sic], lack of joy. In particular, it had to study the 'pathology of normalcy' – the chronic low-grade schizophrenia which is generated in the cybernated, technological society of today and tomorrow.[26] Similarly, David Ingleby has argued that the task of a radical psychoanalysis is 'to show how crippling compulsions arise in the course of *normal* socialisation, and persist because they serve so well the maintenance of oppressive institutions'.[27]

It is the challenge of Fenichel and others to continue this form of analysis, connecting the clinical with the social and political, to move beyond the general statement to the specific. What, precisely, is the relationship of the psychological problems that bring individuals to seek psychotherapy (or indeed not) and the social and political organisation in which they are formed? How are this person's panic attacks, that person's obsessions, this one's despair, that one's paranoia, connected to the social context? To answer this, or at least to think seriously about it – this is part of the task of the psychotherapist who wishes to be engaged in and with the world.

But the political Freudians, and the other early psychoanalysts, did not stop at analysing problems. Many of them, Ferenczi, Reich and Fenichel in particular, were active too in working for political change in the light of the difficulties that their patients brought to them, notably in the area of sexual law reform. This reforming impulse is also evident in a considerable body of British research, much of it associated with the Tavistock Clinic in London, which has been particularly influential on the provision of social services and the delivery of health care especially with regard to children. It has contributed, in the words of Michael Rustin, to a 'broader and richer conception of "social justice" in many important and often indirect ways'.[28]

So too the political Freudians were also active in spreading the availability of psychoanalytic treatment to those who could not afford to pay and who might not encounter it. With Freud's support, Max Eitington and Ernst Simmel founded the Berlin Psychoanalytic Institute to provide psychoanalytic treatment for the less than rich. Jacoby remarks:

> Later, in language never again used by established psychoanalysis, Eitington bemoaned the decline of 'authentic proletarian elements' and the rise of bourgeois intellectuals among Institute patients.[29]

In our own lifetimes, psychotherapists in Latin America, living under repressive regimes, were forced to make the connection between their patients' material and the reality of the world outside the consulting room, although a great many tried to deny such connections.[30] So too Marie Langer wrote of how she and her colleagues who left the Argentine Psychoanalytical Association in the late 1960s finally 'lost our phobia of the world outside our institution'.[31]

At the same time, there is much important work to be done in fostering a spirit of self-reflectiveness about psychoanalytic theory, in engaging in an internal critique of psychotherapeutic theory, in making explicit the implicit assumptions and norms of psychoanalytic theory and practice. A fine example of this is Noreen O'Connor and Joanna Ryan's book on lesbianism and psychoanalysis which interrogates a range of psychoanalytic positions and puts into question a number of assumptions too often taken for granted.[32]

PSYCHOTHERAPY AND THE PROJECT OF AUTONOMY

Although it is not some form of political education or con-sciousness-raising, the practice of psychotherapy has – or can have – a profound political meaning. No one interrogated and articulated this question more trenchantly than the thinker and psychoanalyst, Cornelius Castoriadis. For Casto-riadis, psychoanalysis – and, by extension, I would argue, any form of psychotherapy worthy of the name – aims at the *autonomy* of the human subject. This autonomy has nothing whatsoever to do with a self-centred individualism that some-times pretends to this condition. It is the state of a human subject which, translating the word literally, makes its own laws, which is self-governing, self-reflexive, self-limiting. Such autonomy is inextricably linked to a wider autonomy of society, a society which makes it own laws, which is self-governing, self-reflexive and self-limiting. Neither can exist without the other: 'Democracy in the full sense can be defined as the regime of collective reflexivity; everything else can be shown to follow from this. And there can be no democracy without democratic individuals and vice versa.' An autono-mous society, that is a truly democratic one, can only exist if there are autonomous individuals; autonomous individuals can exist only within the context of an autonomous society. Autonomy is to be contrasted with heteronomy where norms, values and laws are not chosen but seen as imposed from without – for instance because they come from God or from tradition – and are not to be put in question in any meaning-ful way. Democratic creation abolishes all 'transcendent sources of signification'. There are no laws, norms, values or meanings which cannot be put into question: '[D]emocratic creation is the creation of unlimited interrogation in all domains: what is the true and the false, what is the just and unjust, what is the good and what is evil, what is the beautiful and the ugly. It is in this that its *reflectiveness* resides.'[33]

An autonomous individual, for Castoriadis, is one who is truly self-reflective, who knows her own desires and wishes – including, particularly, those that are unconscious – and is prepared to take responsibility for these. In this respect, Castoriadis rewrites the well-known Freudian statement about the aim of psychoanalysis, 'Where id was, there ego shall be.' For Castoriadis, this formulation is 'impossible and monstrous'.[34] It is impossible because there could not be a human being whose unconscious is conquered by the con-scious, whose drives are fully controlled by rational consider-ations, 'who has stopped fantasising and dreaming'. It is monstrous, because to reach such a state would mean to kill what is human; 'this is not rationality, but the uncontrolled and uncontrollable continuous urge of creative radical imagination in and through the flux of representations, affects and desires'. Castoriadis proposes a reformulation, 'Where I [Ego] am (is), That [Id] should/ought also to emerge.' The object of analysis or therapy is not to eliminate one psychical *instanz* (agency) to the profit of another, but rather to alter the relation *between* 'agencies', and to do this it has to alter essentially one of these, the ego or the conscious. 'The ego has to become a self-reflexive subjectivity, capable of deliber-ation and will.' This transformation of the subject can only come about through the process of self-questioning and self-reflectiveness that is psychotherapy.

An autonomous human subject knows, is aware of, her desires, whether or not she chooses to act on them. It is not that psychotherapy can get rid of particular desires or thoughts which we might wish not to have – for instance to murder someone – but that we accept responsibility for these, able to say, 'This is also me.'

Castoriadis couches his thought in Freudian terms, albeit a highly innovative thinking through of Freud, but the general point he is making holds true – or can do – even for those who do not hold to this particular way of seeing. Psychotherapy does not teach a meaning for life. But it can help the patient to find, invent and create for herself such a meaning. Therapy does not bring, as such, happiness, but in bringing neurotic misery to an end it helps the patient to form her own project for life. In particular, Castoriadis argues, analysis or maturity is only achieved when the subject has become able to live 'on the edge of the abyss within this ultimate double bind: live as a mortal, live as if you were immortal. He adds: 'One of the main difficulties, if not *the* main difficulty facing the project of autonomy is the difficulty encountered by human beings in accepting, *sans phrase*, the mortality of the individual, of the collectivity and even of their works.'

Psychoanalysis, for Castoriadis, belongs fully to 'the great social-historical stream of, and struggle for autonomy, in the emancipatory project to which democracy and philosophy also belong.' A psychotherapy that wishes to renew itself, to find its proper political and ethical place in the world, has to remain true to this source.

8

'Where in the waste
is the wisdom?'

It seems to me that we can also say of other institutions that they have ceased to live when they show themselves incapable of carrying on a poetry of human relations – that is, the call of each individual freedom to all the others.

Maurice Merleau-Ponty[1]

But by writing thithaways end to end and turning, turning and end to end hithaways writing and with lines of litters slittering up and louds of letters slittering down, the old semetomyplace and jupetbackagain, from tham Let Rise till Hum Lit. Sleep, where in the waste is the wisdom?

James Joyce[2]

I began this book by saying that it was written partly to answer the question, 'What kind of psychotherapist are you?' Some years ago, long before the book had been conceived, I found myself answering this question by saying that I was a sceptical therapist. This answer wasn't meant to sound flip to my questioner, although it may have done so (it did, slightly, to me). Rather, unknown to myself, I was stumbling into an important realisation. I did not, at the time, really know the meaning of scepticism at least in its philosophical sense, a sense which has come to seem more and more important as time passes.

As I said in the introduction, the kind of scepticism that I am advocating for the practice of psychotherapy has nothing to do with a position that maintains that we can know nothing or that there is no such thing as truth. This is a dangerous position. It is not just that there are truths which may be relatively unimportant, for example that I am sitting at a table writing this, that it is raining outside, that everyone else in the house is asleep. But there are also historical, political or social truths – the Holocaust *did happen*, the war in the former Yugoslavia *did happen*, the Gulf War (contrary to Baudrillard's hallucinations) *did take place* – and these are important truths. Of course, the causes of these events, their parameters and their meaning are all things that can be discussed and contested, but that they happened cannot and it is dangerous nonsense, not to say insulting to those who took part and who suffered, to think they can.

FOR A SCEPTICAL THERAPY

> *At the foundation of well-founded belief lies belief that is not well-founded.*
>
> Ludwig Wittgenstein[3]

> *Language is in itself already scepticism.*
>
> Emmanuel Levinas[4]

> *Most men do not think things in the way they encounter them, nor do they recognise what they experience, but believe their own opinions.*
>
> Heraclitus

The kind of scepticism I am advocating is concerned precisely with truth and is concerned to uncover untruths or to expose pseudo-truths. It is not a method to be applied but rather an attitude, a position.[5] The emphasis in scepticism, at least in the variation propounded by Sextus Empiricus (*c.* AD 200), in on 'thinking rather than on thoughts', its way of seeking is that of questioning and discontinuity. Its aim is therapy because it is addressed to a person in a state of conflict or confusion: 'Empty is that philosopher's argument,' wrote Sextus Empiricus, 'by which no human suffering is therapeutically treated. For just as there is no use in a medical art that does not cast out the sicknesses of bodies, so too there is no use in philosophy, unless it casts out the suffering of the soul.'[6]

The word sceptic derives from the Greek *skeptikos* meaning 'thoughtful', 'reflective', 'paying attention to'. It was motivated by the urgency of human suffering and its goal was that of human flourishing (*eudaimonia*).[7] Scepticism, as Martha Nussbaum shows, was part of that tradition of Hellenistic ethics which combined 'immersion with critical distance . . . insisting on the rigorous scrutiny of belief and desire'. Its investigative process involved a tentative diagnosis of what ailed the person concerned, a tentative norm of health and a conception of proper method. Around two thousand years before the invention of psychoanalysis, the Hellenistic philosophers (including the Sceptics) had also recognised the existence of unconscious motivations and beliefs.[8]

Scepticism is not a technique but an ability – an ability, as Sextus Empiricus put it, 'to set up oppositions among things which appear and are thought of in any way at all, an ability by which, because of the equipollence in the opposed objects and accounts, we come first to the suspension of judgement and afterwards to tranquillity.'[9]

Most modern theories of psychotherapy, John Heaton has argued, are open to criticism from a sceptical position: 'They write as instructors, as people who know and expect their readers to blindly follow them. They rarely question their basic beliefs but assume them and form a school around them. In no way do they encourage the reader to stop and question what is written let alone help him become aware of how words must fall silent in order to mean.' Freud and others repeatedly confuse their beliefs and theories with the phenomena they seek to explain; they obliterate the distinction between conceptual and factual investigation. They engage in circular reasoning in that they use clinical observations from analytic sessions to support their theories not realising that their observations and methods of treatment are dependent on their theories – 'the theory cannot be an adequate explanation of the phenomena'.[10]

There are, in any case, hundreds of different schools of therapy. None of them has any claim to better clinical efficacy than any of the others and despite attempts at eclecticism each clings to its own belief in its own truth. Yet theories of psychotherapy are, as I argued in Chapter 1, imaginative constructs or metaphors; they are not empirical truths, so it is misleading and dangerous to erect systems of belief or pseudo-knowledge upon them. The many different systems of psychotherapy cannot also all be true in any usual sense of the word.

By contrast the sceptic does not diagnose disease in terms of an underlying cause or structure. Rather, the sceptic attends to the state of conflict and allows this to be indicative of its own treatment. 'He attends to where the shoe pinches,' as John Heaton puts it. For the sceptic it would be dogmatic to assert that there is a condition such as hysteria or schizophrenia which underlies the conflict and must be treated by some standard method. At best these diagnostic words are 'commemorative signs' which may be useful to remind us that there are certain similarities between groups of people in conflict. But that there are indicative signs in these people which point to an underlying structure causing the condition is a result of false reasoning.[11]

157

The sceptics are inquirers but this is not the same as to seek, for in inquiry there is no end to be gained and held. Sceptical inquiry does not seek answers.

This kind of scepticism informed the thinking which led to the founding of the Philadelphia Association. An early PA brochure, Robin Cooper notes, quoted from Montaigne: 'For it needs some degree of knowledge to observe that we do not know . . . I, who pretend nothing else, find in myself such an infinite depth and variety that the sole fruit of my study is to make me feel how much I still have to learn.'[12] And R. D. Laing, one of the founders of the Association, himself placed himself very much in the sceptical tradition. In an interview he stressed the importance to him of not trying to supply a lack of knowledge – 'the gaps in what I really know from my immediate direct sight, sound, taste, touch, smell' – not to fill the gaps by beliefs 'one then has to defend since they are imperilled. That's the beginning of fanaticism, and I attribute a great deal of the world's woes to that propensity I recognise in my own mind, and that of other people, to become convinced that one is right, that the questions are finally answered.' Laing connected such a position to that of Keats's negative capability which I spoke of earlier, the ability to live in uncertainty.[13]

Scepticism requires us to put things in question. It opens us to examine whatever it is we take for granted. It requires us, it allows us to wonder at things, a capacity that too many psychotherapists, bored with their work, as Bion once remarked, have lost.[14] It is not that we disavow understanding or meaning – a therapy that did not seek to help people make some sense of their lives would be pointless – but that we recognise that meaning is never fixed for all time, but changes, shifts, is lost, found, forgotten, superseded, and that we seek to keep such understanding and meaning always open and open to question and revision, never foreclosed.

THE GETTING OF WISDOM

*Men who love wisdom must be good inquirers
into many things indeed.*

Heraclitus

If we move beyond or away from the idea that there can be knowledge of the human subject, where are we left? Let us return here to Levinas. What is counterposed to knowledge, Levinas argues, is not ignorance, as most people might say, but rather wisdom. Knowledge, at least in this context, involves siezing something and making it one's own; it appropriates and grasps the otherness of what is known. Beyond knowledge and its hold on being, Levinas argues, lies 'a more urgent form' of meaning, wisdom. Wisdom is inextricably linked to the idea of responsibility to and for the other and the relationship of the face to face, a responsibility which has nothing whatsoever to do with knowledge, indeed which exists prior to any knowledge.[15]

What then is wisdom? Wisdom is something other than knowledge. One may know a great deal and yet not be wise. Indeed, we might say that this is a common condition today. There are many knowledgeable people, many experts in their field, yet few of them we would describe as wise. Wisdom is also about understanding the limitations of knowledge, both the limits of what one knows and the limits of the usefulness of such knowledge. It involves an ability to understand what one knows, to know what it means. 'We had the experience but missed the meaning,' Eliot writes in what we might think of as the opposite of wisdom.[16] It is also the ability to live in uncertainty, to doubt all the time and yet not to be paralysed by such doubt. It is about an ability or capacity to think for oneself, not in the sense of disregarding what has gone before, or of reinventing the wheel, but of somehow making what

159

exists one's own, of speaking with and through one's own voice. But again wisdom isn't just about thinking or thought either. It is not the exercise of some intellectual capacity. It requires a real sensitivity to others, a fine judgement, an ethical sense. And while having nothing to do with chronological age, wisdom is inescapably about experience; a young man might be wise for his years but his wisdom will inevitably be limited by his age.

In terms of the practice of psychotherapy, wisdom means being able to see each person as he really is, to suspend one's preconceptions, and to bring to bear one's experience, at the same time not losing sight of the fact that what one is seeing before one is another, utterly individual human being, different from and irreducible to all the others as to any general theorising. It involves an ability to be truly open to the other, not to try and fit him into any preconceived model or theory. It requires an ability too to learn from experience, not in the sense that one knows more facts but rather that one's conception of and thoughts about the world have been broadened. (There is, as Eliot cautioned, only a limited value in the knowledge gained from experience, for such knowledge 'imposes a pattern, and falsifies'. We have to remember that 'the pattern is new in every moment/And every moment is a new and shocking/Valuation of all we have been.'[17]) It is a position which does not *tolerate* unknowing or uncertainty, for that implies a passing phase, something to be got through or got over, but which welcomes such unknowing and uncertainty as the ground from which something worthwhile might emerge.

In psychotherapy, wisdom is not about knowledge any more than in any other field. It is, in any case, questionable what kind of knowledge there can be in psychotherapy, perhaps, as Eliot says, 'only the knowledge of dead secrets/ useless in the darkness into which they peered'.[18] It is not that the wise therapist *knows* more than others but that he has a particular way of being with others and of thinking about and with them. It is this quality, I believe, this way of being, of respect, of attentiveness and of attunement, that marks out the great psychotherapists, whatever their particular theoretical position, from the rest.

Above all, perhaps, wisdom involves humility, a humility in the face of the utter complexity of what it means to be human and in the face of human suffering, whatever its degree, a humility in the limits of what can be done. 'Do not let me hear of the wisdom of old men,' Eliot says in 'East Coker', 'but rather of their folly, their fear of fear and frenzy . . . The only wisdom we can hope to acquire is the wisdom of humility: humility is endless.'[19]

The position that I have been advocating in this book, whether we think of it in terms of scepticism or the *via negativa* or negative capability, in no way is a guarantee of truth or of giving us access to some kind of pure and unadulterated experience. Rather, like all positions we adopt, it requires to be accompanied by a belief that whatever understanding we come to is inevitably provisional, subject always to further inquiry, modification and revision. There can be no finality. To quote Beckett once again, we fail again but we fail better. This is as true of Levinas's position, to which I have given so much emphasis in this book, as it is to any other. An ethical stance does not bestow on us a privileged position; truthfulness is not guaranteed. The ethical stance must be combined with a scepticism if it is not to reify into dogma, if it is to remain respectful of the other and truly responsible and truly ethical.

THERAPY AS FRIENDSHIP

> *A friend is a person with whom I may be sincere.*
> *Before him I may think aloud.*
> Ralph Waldo Emerson[20]

The ethical stance of psychotherapy that I have been advocating might well take as a model, if it needs one, that of
friendship. (I am here following through a remark made by
Adam Phillips that therapy, or at least the kind of therapy he
is interested in, is 'closer to friendship than to a doctor-
patient relationship'.[21]) Perhaps we might think of therapy as
a *form* of friendship. As soon as I say this I know that we are
here on dangerous territory and immediately anxieties rise. I
shall be accused of suggesting that therapists invite their
patients or clients to the cinema, for a meal, to ring up and
discuss a television programme, to give us presents on our
birthdays and so on. 'What about boundaries?' it will be
objected. Of course, the word to be emphasised here is 'form'
– not all friendships are the same. So too does friendship have
its own boundaries and conventions, albeit highly complex
and shifting. It is a grave injustice to think of friendship as
something trivial, or something 'nice' that serves only to
gratify each party to it. This is to make the mistake, once
again, of seeing in the ordinary something unworthy of
attention whereas it is, in truth, something highly complex
and often immensely confusing.

How dismissive we are, contemptuous even, when people
who know little of therapy say that it sounds like talking to a
friend or that instead of paying a therapist one should talk to
one's friends. There is, perhaps, rather more to such remarks
than ignorance. I think such statements reveal a belief in what
friends *should* be able to do, what friendship *might* consist of
– and what it too often does not. Think of the elements of a

good friend – someone who has our interests at heart, who has a sense of our history and who respects us, who does not suspend criticism but who is nevertheless tactful, who can stand back from what we are describing, who can talk honestly and openly to us, who has time for us, who is attentive and thoughtful and appreciative and who can keep his own feelings out of, say, any predicament that we might be describing. An ideal type indeed, but are not these the qualities, or some of them, of a good therapist? I believe they are. There is a major difference, of course. A social friendship that did not involve a degree of reciprocity over time would be unsustainable and a lack of reciprocity is, I suspect, why so many friendships founder on a reef of resentment of one kind or another. Therapy on the other hand, to return to Levinas, is not reciprocal. I am there for the other; he is not there for me but this does not make it any less a friendship and it does not preclude a reciprocity if this seems appropriate, in the sense of a sharing of one's experience or thought. And, of course, friendship is a struggle and a challenge, for both parties, not just in the negotiation of the boundaries and form but in a more fundamental respect which is to do with whether one wants or can even tolerate the closeness and intimacy offered.

And yet all the qualities of a good friendship – a welcome, an acceptance, a letting be, a hospitality, an attunement, an attentiveness, a suspension of self-interest, a questioning, a criticism, a distance that does not yet pretend to objectivity, an engagement, a faith in the other, a commitment to truthfulness, and above all perhaps a responsibility to the other – these surely are the qualities also of an ethical therapy. In the end, however, these can no more be a guide than there could be a guide to friendship. The content of therapy, the form of a particular therapeutic relationship – these *are* the ethical challenge, the challenge of responsibility, a responsibility without end.

Notes

Introduction

1. MIT Press, Massachussetts, 1994.
2. p. 7.
3. Walter Benjamin too, according to Hannah Arendt, wanted to write a book consisting entirely of quotations. For him, the function of quotations was not to verify and document opinions, as it was for other scholars: 'The main work consisted in tearing fragments out of their context and arranging them afresh in such a way that they illustrated one another and were able to prove their *raison d'être* in a free-floating state as it were.' ('Introduction', Benjamin, W., *Illuminations* (trans. H. Zohn), Jonathan Cape, London, 1970, p. 47.)
4. See, for instance, *True and False Experience: the human element in psychotherapy* (Allen Lane, London, 1973), *The Limits of Interpretation* (Penguin, Harmondsworth, 1987) and *Cultivating Intuition: an introduction to psychotherapy* (Penguin, London, 1994).
5. Jonathan Cape, London, 1997, p. 27.

Notes

Chapter 1

1. *The Death of the Family*, Allen Lane, Harmondsworth, 1971, p. 45.
2. Letter to Oskar Pfister, quoted in Rieff, P., *The Triumph of the Therapeutic: uses of truth after Freud*, Chatto and Windus, London, 1966, p. 107.
3. 'What We Talk about When We Talk about Love', *Where I'm Calling From: the selected stories*, Harvill, London, 1993.
4. 'What we take for granted', *Free Associations*, Vol. 6, Part 4, No. 40, 1997, p. 544.
5. Bion, W. R., *Bion in New York and Sao Paolo*, Clunie Press, Perthshire, 1980, pp. 94–5.
6. *Cultivating Intuition: an introduction to psychotherapy*, Penguin, London, 1994, p. 21.
7. *Psychoanalysis and Beyond*, Chatto and Windus, London, 1985, p. 10.
8. See Castoriadis, C., 'Psychoanalysis and philosophy', *The Castoriadis Reader* (Curtis, D.A. ed.), Blackwell, Oxford, 1997, p. 349.
9. 'Why am I here?', *The Baby and the Bathwater*, Karnac Books, London, 1996, p. 33.
10. Eisold, K., 'The intolerance of diversity in psychoanalytic institutes', *International Journal of Psycho-Analysis*, Vol. 75, 1994, pp. 785–90.
11. 'From Hiroshima to the Gulf War and after: a psychoanalytic perspective' in *Psychoanalysis in Contexts: paths between theory and modern culture* (Elliott, A. and Frosh, S. eds.), Routledge, London, 1995, p. 191.
12. *Freud and Man's Soul*, Chatto and Windus, London, 1983, p. 5.
13. Bouveresse, J., *Wittgenstein reads Freud: the myth of the*

165

unconscious (trans. C. Cosman), Princeton University Press, Princeton, 1995, p. xii.

14. Quoted in *Wittgenstein reads Freud*, p. 7.
15. 'What is science? What is psychoanalysis? What is to be done?', *British Journal of Pychotherapy*, Vol. 13, No. 1, 1996.
16. 'On psychoanalysis, talmudism, and anything-goesism', unpublished lecture, 1997.
17. *Against Method: outline of an anarchistic theory of knowledge*, Verso, London, 1975, p. 23.
18. *The Voice of Experience: experience, science and society*, Penguin, Harmondsworth, 1983, p. 41.
19. *Psychiatry and Anti-Psychiatry*, Tavistock Publications, London, 1967, p. 39.
20. *Disabling Professions*, Marion Boyars, London, 1977, p. 15.
21. 'Professionalised service and disabling help', *Disabling Professions*, p. 74.
22. Orbach, S., *What's Really Going on Here?*, Virago, London, 1994, p. 102.
23. *Finnegans Wake*, Faber and Faber, London, 1939, p. 76.
24. *Bion in New York and Sao Paolo*, Clunie Press, Perthshire, 1980, p. 14.
25. *Clinical Seminars and Other Works*, Karnac Books, London, 1994, p. 74.
26. *The Politics of Experience and the Bird of Paradise*, Penguin, Harmondsworth, 1967, p. 15.
27. Quoted in *London Review of Books*, 8 May 1997. Thompson also, of course, lambasted with great wit, if at great length, the notion of theory, at least in the over-arching, over-bearing sense given it by so-called 'scientific Marxists' such as Louis Althusser and others, in the title essay of *The Poverty of Theory and other essays*, Merlin, London, 1978, which ought to be read by all psychotherapists.

28. Quoted in Hinshelwood, R. D., *A Dictionary of Kleinian Thought*, Free Association Books, London, 1991, p. 330.
29. *Illness as Metaphor/Aids and Its Metaphors*, Penguin, London, 1983, p. 91.
30. *Phenomenology of Perception* (trans. C. Smith), Routledge and Kegan Paul, London, 1962, p. xi.
31. *Phenomenology of Perception*, p. 158.
32. 'Introducing an incomplete project', *Between Philosophy and Psychoanalysis: papers from the Philadelphia Association*, Cooper, R. and others, Free Association Books, London, 1989, p. 4.
33. 'Epilogue', *Day by Day*, Faber and Faber, London, 1978, p. 127.
34. Pedder, J., 'Some biographical contributions to psychoanalytic theories', *Free Associations*, No. 10, 1987.
35. Basic Books, New York, 1983.
36. 'Psychoanalysis and politics', *World in Fragments: writings on politics, society, psychoanalysis and the imagination* (Curtis, D. A. ed. and trans.), Stanford University Press, Stanford, 1997, p. 135.
37. Berman, M., *All that is Solid Melts into Air: the experience of modernity*, Verso, London, 1982, p. 35.
38. 'The Greek polis and the creation of democracy', *Philosophy, Politics, Autonomy* (Curtis, D. A. ed. and trans.), Oxford University Press, Oxford, 1991, p. 88.
39. Obituary, *Guardian*, 24 January 1996.
40. In *Sweeping Out the Dark*, Carcanet, Manchester, 1994, p. 42.

Notes

Chapter 2

1. Wright, T., Hughes, P. and Ainley, A., 'The paradox of morality: an interview with Emmanuel Levinas', *The Provocation of Levinas: rethinking the other* (Bernasconi, R. and Wood, D. eds), Routledge, London, 1988, p. 172.
2. Quoted in Bauman, Z., *Postmodern Ethics*, Blackwell, Oxford, 1993, p. 49.
3. Quoted in Kearney, R., *The Wake of Imagination*, Hutchinson, London, 1988, p. 365.
4. 'The paradox of morality: an interview with Emmanuel Levinas', p. 97.
5. Bauman, Z., *Life in Fragments: essays in postmodern morality*, Blackwell, Oxford, 1995, p. 268.
6. Mortley, R., *French Philosophers in Conversation*, Routledge, London, 1991, p. 16.
7. Bauman, Z., *Postmodern Ethics*, p. 50.
8. 'Substitution', *The Levinas Reader* (Hand, S. ed.) Blackwell, Oxford, 1989, p. 104.
9. Quoted in Gans, S., 'Levinas and the question of the group' in Oakley, C. (ed.), *What is a Group?*, Rebus Press, London, forthcoming.
10. 'The paradox of morality: an interview with Emmanuel Levinas', p. 169.
11. Kearney, R., *Dialogues with Contemporary Continental Thinkers*, Manchester University Press, Manchester, 1989, p. 60.
12. 'The paradox of morality: an interview with Emmanuel Levinas', p. 170.
13. 'The paradox of morality: an interview with Emmanuel Levinas', p. 169.
14. Vetlese, A.J. quoted in Bauman, Z., *Life in Fragments*, p. 53.
15. Bauman, Z., *Postmodern Ethics*, pp. 48–9.

16. Rée, J., 'Selflessness', *London Review of Books*, 8 May 1997, pp. 16–19.
17. Mortley, R., *French Philosophers in Conversation*, Routledge, London, 1991, p. 15.
18. Bauman, Z., *Life in Fragments*, p. 64.
19. Quoted in Bauman, Z., *Postmodern Ethics*, p. 79.
20. Quoted in Bauman, Z., *Life in Fragments*, p. 56.
21. Bauman, Z., *Life in Fragments*, p. 56, emphasis added.
22. Bauman, Z., *Life in Fragments*, p. 57.
23. Bauman, Z., *Life in Fragments*, p. 65.
24. Sereny, G., *Albert Speer: his battle with truth*, Macmillan, London, 1995.
25. 'The paradox of morality: an interview with Emmanuel Levinas', pp. 169–70.
26. Kearney, R., *Dialogues with Contemporary Continental Thinkers*, Manchester University Press, Manchester, 1989, pp. 64–5.
27. Critchley, S., *The Ethics of Deconstruction: Derrida and Levinas*, Blackwell, Oxford, 1993, p. 7.
28. 'The servant and her master', *The Levinas Reader* (Hand, S. ed.), Blackwell, Oxford, 1989, pp. 156–7.
29. Critchley, S., *The Ethics of Deconstruction: Derrida and Levinas*, p. 7.
30. Heaton, J., 'The other and psychotherapy', *The Provocation of Levinas: rethinking the other* (Bernasconi, R. and Wood, D. eds), p. 6.
31. Gans, S., 'Levinas and Pontalis: meeting the other as in a dream', *The Provocation of Levinas: rethinking the other* (Bernasconi, R. and Wood, D. eds.), p. 86.
32. Gans, S., 'Levinas and the question of the group' in Oakley, C. (ed.), *What is a Group?*, Rebus Press, London, forthcoming.

Chapter 3

1. 'Chocorua to its neighbour', *Collected Poems*, Faber and Faber, London, 1955, p. 296.
2. *Phenomenology of Perception* (trans. C. Smith), Routledge and Kegan Paul, London, 1962, p. 187.
3. 'Indirect language and the voices of silence', *Signs* (trans. R. McCleary), Northwestern University Press, Evanston, 1964, pp. 42–3.
4. Quoted in Sampson, E., *Celebrating the Other: a dialogic account of human nature*, Harvester, Hemel Hempstead, 1993, p. 108.
5. 'Indirect language and the voices of silence', pp. 42–3.
6. *Phenomenology of Perception*, p. 193.
7. Quoted in Todorov, T., *Mikhail Bakhtin: The Dialogical Principle* (trans. W. Godzich), University of Minnesota Press, Minneapolis, 1984, p. 116.
8. *Real Presences*, Faber and Faber, London, 1989, p. 226.
9. 'The person', *The Category of the Person: anthropology, philosophy, history* (Carrithers, M., Collins, S. and Lukes, S. eds.), Cambridge University Press, Cambridge, 1985, p. 273.
10. 'Indirect language and the voices of silence', p. 43, emphasis added.
11. Quoted in *Phenomenology of Perception*, p. 196.
12. 'Building, dwelling, thinking', *Poetry, Language, Thought* (trans. A. Hofstadter), Harper and Row, New York, 1971, p. 146.
13. *Mikhail Bakhtin: The Dialogical Principle*, p. 97.
14. *Mikhail Bakhtin: The Dialogical Principle*, p. 44.
15. *Mikhail Bakhtin: The Dialogical Principle*, p. 30.
16. Quoted in Sampson, *Celebrating the Other*, p. 135.
17. *Freudianism: a critical sketch* (trans. I. R. Titunik), Indiana University Press, Bloomington, 1976, p. 79. I follow

the generally accepted notion that Bakhtin was either the sole or main author of this work attributed to V. N. Volosinov.

18. *Marxism and the Philosophy of Language*, p. 86, quoted in Sampson, *Celebrating the Other*, p. 134.

19. Quoted in *Mikhail Bakhtin: The Dialogical Principle*, p. 116.

20. *Seeing Voices: a journey into the world of the deaf*, Pan, London, 1991, p. 45.

21. *Freudianism: a critical sketch*, p. 79.

22. *Freudianism: a critical sketch*, p. 80.

23. *Mikhail Bakhtin: The Dialogical Principle*, p. 32.

24. Sampson, *Celebrating the Other*, p. 108.

25. Sampson, *Celebrating the Other*, p. 104.

26. *The Other Side of Language: a philosophy of listening* (trans. C. Lambert), Routledge, London, 1990.

27. *The Other Side of Language*, pp. 30–31.

28. Wright, T., Hughes, P., and Ainley, A., 'The paradox of morality: an interview with Emmanuel Levinas', *The Provocation of Levinas: rethinking the other* (Bernasconi, R. and Wood, D. eds.), Routledge, London, 1988, p. 170.

29. Quoted in Sampson, *Celebrating the Other*, p. 136.

30. *Early Greek Thinking*, quoted in *The Other Side of Language*, p. 31.

31. *Truth and Method*, quoted in *The Other Side of Language*, p. 28.

32. *The Other Side of Language*, p. 189.

33. *The Other Side of Language*, p. 189.

34. *Truth and Method*, quoted in *The Other Side of Language*, p. 189.

35. Klein, M., 'The importance of symbol formation in the development of the ego' (1930), *The Selected Melanie Klein* (Mitchell, J. ed.), Penguin, London, 1986, pp. 102–3.

36. *Mikhail Bakhtin: The Dialogical Principle*, p. 52.

37. *Phenomenology of Perception*, p. 187.
38. Mortley, R., *French Philosophers in Conversation*, Routledge, London, 1991, pp. 37–9.
39. *Double Vision: my life in film*, Faber and Faber, London, 1989, p. 82.
40. 'Kandinsky's Ribbons', *Aimed at Nobody*, Faber and Faber, London, 1993.
41. 'The task of the translator', *Illuminations* (trans. H. Zohn), Collins, Glasgow, 1970.
42. Quoted in May, R., *The Courage to Create*, Bantam Books, New York, 1975, p. 163.
43. 'The eloquence of silence', *Celebration of Awareness: a call for institutional revolution*, Penguin, Harmondsworth, 1973, p. 41.
44. 'The eloquence of silence', p. 42.
45. 'The eloquence of silence', pp. 41–2.
46. *Everyday Life* (trans. G. L. Campbell), Routledge and Kegan Paul, London, 1984, p. 227.
47. Kane, L., *The Language of Silence*, quoted in Cox, M. and Theilgard, A., *Mutative Metaphors in Psychotherapy: the aeolian mode*, Tavistock Publications, London, 1987, p. 4.
48. *On Dialogue*, David Bohm Seminars, Ojai, California, 1990, pp. 1–2, 14.
49. Gadamer, H. G., *Truth and Method*, p. 330, quoted in *The Other Side of Language*, p. 36.
50. *Cultivating Intuition: an introduction to psychotherapy*, Penguin, London, 1994, p. 198.
51. 'What analysts say to their patients', *Psychoanalysis and Beyond*, Chatto and Windus, London, 1985, pp. 62–3.
52. 'What analysts say to their patients', pp. 62–3.
53. 'An enquiry into the function of words in the analytic situation', *The British School of Psychoanalysis: the independent tradition* (Kohon, G. ed.), Free Association Books, London, 1986, pp. 243–4.

54. 'Child analysis in the latency period' (1958), *The Maturational Processes and the Facilitating Environment*, Hogarth Press, London, 1965, p. 122.

Chapter 4

1. *Ethics and Infinity: conversations with Philippe Nemo* (trans. R. A. Cohen), Duquesne University Press, Pittsburgh, 1985, p. 115.
2. I have borrowed the phrase from Stephen Kurtz's book, *The Art of Unknowing: dimensions of openness in analytic therapy*, Jason Aronson, New York, 1989, to which I am indebted.
3. *The Writing of the Disaster* (trans. A. Smock), University of Nebraska Press, Lincoln and London, 1986, p. 59.
4. Friedman, J., 'Therapeia, play and the therapeutic household', *Thresholds Between Philosophy and Psychoanalysis: papers from the Philadelphia Association* (Cooper. R. and others), Free Association Books, London, 1989, p. 57.
5. 'Therapeia, play and the therapeutic household', p. 63.
6. 'Therapeia, play and the therapeutic household', p. 70.
7. 'Time sequences, continuity of movement', *The Logic of Images: essays and conversations* (trans. M. Hoffman), Faber and Faber, London, 1991, p. 4.
8. *Guardian*, 31 March 1993.
9. *The Infinite Conversation* (trans. S. Hanson), University of Minnesota Press, Minneapolis and London, 1993, p. 121.
10. *Postmodern Ethics*, Blackwell, Oxford, 1993, p. 87.
11. *Brazilian Lectures*, Karnac Books, London, 1990, p. 5.
12. *Bion in New York and Sao Paolo*, Clunie Press, Perthshire, 1980, p. 11.
13. *Bion in New York and Sao Paolo*, p. 34.

14. *Playing and Reality*, Penguin, Harmondsworth, 1971, pp. 102–3.
15. *The Art of Unknowing*, p. 4.
16. *Brazilian Lectures*, p. 29.
17. *Brazilian Lectures*, p. 88.
18. *The Art of Unknowing*, p. 7.
19. *The Art of Unknowing*, pp. 162–3.
20. *Reasons for Knocking at an Empty House: writings 1973–1994*, Thames and Hudson, London, 1995, p. 249.
21. *Reasons for Knocking at an Empty House*, p. 250.
22. Quoted in *Reasons for Knocking at an Empty House*, p. 117.
23. 'East Coker', *Four Quartets*, Faber and Faber, London, 1944, p. 29.
24. Letter to George and Thomas Keats, 21 December 1817, quoted in Bion, W. R., *Attention and Interpretation*, Karnac Books, London, 1970, p. 125.
25. Quoted in Steiner, G., *Real Presences*, Faber and Faber, London, 1989, p. 224.
26. *The Infinite Conversation*, p. 13.
27. *The Infinite Conversation*, p. 54, my emphasis.
28. 'Wanda', *Facing the River*, Carcanet, Manchester, 1995, p. 53.
29. See on this particularly Felman, S. and Laub, D., *Testimony: crises of witnessing in literature, psychoanalysis and history*, Routledge, London, 1992, but also the impressive poetry collection *Against Forgetting: twentieth century poetry of witness* (Forché, C. ed.), W. W. Norton, New York, 1993.
30. Quoted in Berger, J., 'Victor Serge', *Selected Essays and Articles: the look of things*, Penguin, Harmondsworth, 1972, p. 75. See also Gordon, P., 'A stranger in no land: remembering Victor Serge', *Race & Class*, Vol. 39, No. 4, 1998, pp. 49–58.

31. *The Drowned and the Saved* (trans. R. Rosenthal), Michael Joseph, London, 1988, pp. 63–4.
32. *If This is a Man/The Truce* (trans. S. Woolf), Penguin, Harmondsworth, 1979, p. 66.
33. *Testimony*, p. 57.
34. *Testimony*, p. 16.
35. *Testimony*, p. 62.
36. 'Ashglory' quoted in Felstiner, P., *Paul Celan: poet, survivor, Jew*, Yale University Press, New Haven and London, 1995, p. 223.
37. *Lives of the Poets*, Michael Joseph, London, 1985.
38. *One Hundred Years of Solitude* (trans. G. Rabassa), Jonathan Cape, London, 1970, pp. 45–6.
39. 'Feeling our way through', *Guardian*, 23 February 1991.
40. Quoted in *The Poetry of Survival: post-war poets of central and eastern Europe* (Weissbort, D. ed.), Penguin, London, 1993, p. 206.
41. Quoted in Auster, P., *Ground Work: selected poems and essays 1970–1979*, Faber and Faber, London, 1990, p. 156.
42. See Taylor, C., *Sources of the Self: the making of modern identity*, Cambridge University Press, Cambridge, 1989, p. 478.

Chapter 5

1. 'In Wartime' (1942).
2. 'Building, dwelling, thinking', *Poetry, Language, Thought* (trans. A. Hofstadter), Harper and Row, New York, 1971, p. 157.
3. *The Production of Space* (trans. D. Nicholson-Smith), Blackwell, Oxford, 1991, p. 35.
4. Berger, P. L., Berger, B. and Kellner, H., *The Homeless*

Mind: modernization and consciousness, Penguin, Harmondsworth, 1974, p. 77.

5. *The Poetics of Space* (trans. M. Jolas), Beacon Press, Boston, 1958, p. 7.
6. 'Where are we at home?', *Thesis Eleven*, No. 41, 1995, pp. 14–15.
7. 'Where are we at home?', p. 15.
8. 'Where are we at home?', p. 5.
9. *Everyday Life* (trans. G. L. Campbell), Routledge and Kegan Paul, London, 1984, p. 239.
10. *Everyday Life*, p. 239.
11. *Totality and Infinity: an essay on exteriority* (trans. A. Lingis), Duquesne University Press, Pittsburgh, 1969, p. 157.
12. *Existence and Existents* (trans. A. Lingis), Kluwer Academic Publishers, Dordrecht, 1978, p. 69.
13. *Totality and Infinity*, pp. 52–3.
14. *Four Quartets*, Faber and Faber, London, 1944, p. 31.
15. *Totality and Infinity*, p. 156.
16. 'Building, dwelling, thinking', p. 147.
17. 'Building, dwelling, thinking', p. 161.
18. 'Building, dwelling, thinking', p. 157.
19. Quoted by Oakley, H., 'The legacy of R. D. Laing', *THERIP Review*, No. 1, 1995, p. 160.
20. 'What we take for granted', *Free Associations*, Vol. 6, Part 4, No. 40, 1997, p. 547.
21. *The Poetics of Space*, p. 11.
22. See Auster, P., *Ground Work: selected poems and essays 1970–1979*, Faber and Faber, London, 1990, p. 148.
23. Cooper, R., 'What we take for granted', p. 547.
24. 'Dwelling and the "therapeutic community"', *Thresholds Between Philosophy and Psychoanalysis: papers from the Philadelphia Association*, Cooper, R., and others, Free Association Books, London, 1989.
25. Eliot, T. S., 'Burnt Norton', *Four Quartets*, p. 15.

26. *Totality and Infinity*, pp. 155–6.
27. 'An enquiry into the function of words in the psychoanalytical situation', *The British School of Psychoanalysis: the independent tradition* (Kohon, G. ed.), Free Association Books, London, 1986.
28. *Playing and Reality*, p. 44.
29. *Playing and Reality*, p. 63.
30. 'Tradition, violence and psychotherapy', *From the Words of My Mouth: tradition in psychotherapy* (Spurling, L. ed.), Routledge, London, 1993, pp. 145 and 152.
31. *The Poetics of Space*, p. 8.
32. *The Poetics of Space*. p. 15.
33. *The Poetics of Space*. pp. 6–7.
34. *The Poetics of Space*. pp. 46–7.
35. *You Can't Go Home Again* (1940), Penguin, Harmondsworth, 1970, p. 641.
36. Eliot, T. S., 'Little Gidding', *Four Quartets*, p. 59.
37. 'What we take for granted', p. 548.
38. In *The Man With the Night Sweats*, Faber and Faber, London, 1992, pp. 19–20.
39. *Totality and Infinity*, p. 70.
40. *Existence and Existents*, p. 82.
41. 'Final soliloquy of the interior paramour', *Collected Poems*, Faber and Faber, London, 1955, p. 524.

Chapter 6

1. *Paterson*, quoted in Hamburger, M., *The Truth of Poetry: tensions in modernist poetry since Baudelaire*, Weidenfeld and Nicholson, London, 1968 (Anvil Press, London, 1996), p. 253.
2. Quoted in Viola, B., *Reasons for Knocking at an Empty House: writings 1973–1994*, Thames and Hudson, London, 1995, p. 67.

3. *The Poetics of Space* (trans. M. Jolas), Beacon Press, Boston, 1958, p. 84.

4. Tavistock Publications, London, 1987.

5. I should like to thank Don Paterson for introducing me to the poetry of W. S. Graham and to the writings of Randall Jarrell and Charles Simic. My debt to Michael Hamburger's *The Truth of Poetry* (see Note 1) is also considerable.

6. 'Little Gidding', *Four Quartets*, Faber and Faber, London, 1944, p. 54.

7. Quoted in Holmes, J., *Between Art and Science: essays in psychotherapy and psychiatry*, Routledge, London, 1993, p. 135.

8. *Collected Poems*, Faber and Faber, London, 1955, p. 239.

9. *Collected Poems*, p. 183.

10. Quoted in Jarrell, R., *Poetry and the Age*, Faber and Faber, London, 1955, p. 215.

11. Quoted in Hamburger, M., *The Truth of Poetry*, p. 249.

12. *The Truth of Poetry*, p. 248. Yet, as Michael Hamburger remarks, even Różewicz had to admit in his work the necessity of the imagination in order to render even such stark realities as starvation and sexual deprivation, 'and beauty, too, may creep in by the back door, because rightness of any kind – especially that which results from the proper adaptation of means to a function – is felt to be beautiful' (pp. 250–1).

13. *Bion in New York and Sao Paolo*, Clunie Press, Perthsire, 1980, p. 17.

14. *Four Quartets*, p. 58.

15. *Selected Poems* (trans. M. Hamburger), Penguin, London, 1990, p. 99.

16. Quoted in Holmes, J., *Between Art and Science: essays in psychotherapy and psychiatry*, p. 138.

17. *Socialism in a Crippled World*, Penguin, Harmondsworth, 1981, p. 105. On Eliot's anti-Semitism see Julius, A., *T. S. Eliot, Anti-Semitism and Literary Form*, Cambridge University Press, Cambridge, 1995.
18. 'Notes on poetry and philosophy', *Wonderful Words, Silent Truth: essays on poetry and a memoir*, University of Michigan Press, Ann Arbor, 1990, pp. 64–5.
19. 'Notes on poetry and philosophy', p. 63.
20. 'An unpublished text', (trans. A. B. Dallery), *The Primacy of Perception*, Northwestern University Press, Evanston, 1964, p. 9.
21. *The Act of Seeing: essays and conversations*, (trans. M. Hoffman), Faber and Faber, London, 1997, pp. 32–3.
22. *The Poetics of Reverie* (trans. D. Russell), Beacon Press, Boston, 1960, p. 149.
23. Quoted in Milner, M., *The Suppressed Madness of Sane Men*, Routledge, London, 1987, p. 207.
24. Quoted in *Aimed at Nobody*, Faber and Faber, London, 1993, p. 10.
25. *Selected Poems*, Faber and Faber, London, 1996, pp. 43–7.
26. *Selected Poems*, p. 50.
27. 'The Constructed Space', *Selected Poems*, p. 50.
28. 'Burnt Norton', *Four Quartets*, p. 19.
29. 'East Coker', *Four Quartets*, p. 26.
30. 'East Coker', pp. 30–31.
31. 'East Coker', p. 31.
32. 'Notes on poetry and philosophy', p. 66.
33. 'Notes on poetry and philosophy', p. 66.
34. Quoted in Reid, A., 'Neruda and Borges', *New Yorker*, 24 June/1 July 1996, p. 64.
35. 'The noble rider and the Sound of words', *The Necessary Angel: essays on reality and the imagination*, Faber and Faber, London, 1960, p. 32.
36. *The Poetics of Reverie*, p. 127.

37. *The Redress of Poetry: Oxford lectures*, Faber and Faber, London, 1995, pp. 4, 15.

38. *The Redress of Poetry*, p. 8.

39. 'Uncommon visage: the Nobel lecture', *On Grief and Reason: essays*, Hamish Hamilton, London, 1996, p. 46.

40. Quoted in *The Redress of Poetry*, p. 193.

41. 'Feelings into words', *Twentieth Century Poetry and Poetics* (Geddes, G. ed.), Oxford University Press, Oxford, 1985, p. 568.

42. 'Notes on poetry and philosophy', p. 68.

43. Quoted in *The Truth of Poetry*, p. 104.

44. 'Notes on poetry and philosophy', p. 65.

45. 'The obscurity of the poet', *Poetry and the Age*, p. 19.

46. 'Culture in a democratic society;, *The Castoriadis Reader* (Curtis, D. A. ed.), Blackwell, Oxford, 1997, p. 346.

47. Like any English-language speaker I am indebted to Michael Hamburger for his translations of Celan's poetry, *Paul Celan: selected poems* (Anvil Press, London, 1988; Penguin, London, 1990), as I am to John Felstiner for his magisterial but always accessible study, *Paul Celan: poet, survivor, Jew* (Yale University Press, New Haven and London, 1995).

48. 'The Meridian', (trans. J. Glenn), *Chicago Review*, Vol. 29, No. 3, winter 1978, pp. 29–40.

49. 'The Meridian', p. 37.

50. 'The Meridian', p. 39.

51. (trans. S. Melville), *Chicago Review*, Vol. 29, No. 3, winter 1978, pp. 16–22; also in *Proper Names* (trans. M. B. Smith), Stanford University Press, Stanford 1996.

52. (trans. A. Lingis), Kluwer Academic Publishers, Dordrecht, 1978, p. 43.

53. 'Marina', *The Complete Poems and Plays*, Faber and Faber, London, 1969, pp. 109–10.

Chapter 7

1. Quoted in Jacoby, R., *Social Amnesia: a critique of conformist psychology from Adler to Laing*, Harvester, Brighton, 1975, p. 8.
2. 'Done and to be done', *The Castoriadis Reader* (Curtis, D. A. ed. and trans.), Blackwell Publishers, Oxford, 1997, p. 417.
3. '"Man is by nature a political animal" or: patient as citizen', *Speculations After Freud: psychoanalysis, philosophy and culture* (Shamdasani, S. and Munchow, M. eds.), Routledge, London, 1994, p. 33.
5. *The Last Intellectuals: American culture in the age of academe*, Basic Books, New York, 1987.
6. *In Theory: classes, nations, literature*, Verso, London, 1992, p. 69.
7. 'The ambivalence of psychoanalysis', *Free Associations*, No. 1, 1984, p. 40.
8. *The Good Society and the Inner World: psychoanalysis, politics and culture*, Verso, London, 1991.
9. *The Political Psyche*, Routledge, London, 1993, p. 9.
10. *The Political Psyche*, pp. 9–10.
11. Gordon, P., 'Souls in armour: thoughts on psychoanalysis and racism', *British Journal of Psychotherapy*, Vol. 10, No. 1, 1993, pp. 62–76.
12. *Wild Desires and Mistaken Identities: lesbianism and psychoanalysis*, Virago, London, 1993.
13. 'Silence is the real crime', *International Review of Psychoanalysis*, Vol. 14, 1987, pp. 3–12.
14. 'The Free Associations interview', *Free Associations*, No. 24, 1992.
15. *The Culture of Narcissism: American life in an age of diminishing expectations*, Sphere Books, London, 1979.

16. See 'The social-historical: mode of being, problem of knowledge', *Philosophy, Politics, Autonomy* (Curtis, D. A. ed. and trans.), Oxford University Press, Oxford, 1991, p.42.
17. *Freud or Reich?: psychoanalysis and illusion* (trans. C. Pajaczkowska), Free Association Books, London, 1986.
18. Miller, E., 'Implications of the changing world of work', *Living Together* (Kennard, D. and Small, N. eds.), Quartet Books, London, 1997, p. 106.
19. *Social Amnesia*, pp. 139–40.
20. 'Remembering Social Amnesia', *Free Associations*, No. 1, 1984, p. 19.
21. (Trans. C. Farrington), Penguin, Harmondsworth, 1965.
22. See Langer, M., 'Psychoanalysis without the couch', *Free Associations*, No. 15, 1989.
23. See Straker, G., 'Child abuse, counselling and apartheid: the work of the Sanctuary Counselling Team', *Free Associations*, No. 14, 1988.
24. Basic Books, New York, 1983.
25. *The Psychoanalytic Theory of Neurosis*, Kegan Paul, London, 1945, p. 586.
26. *The Crisis of Psychoanalysis: essays on Freud, Marx and social psychology*, Holt, Rinehart and Winston, New York, 1970, pp. 16, 40–1.
27. 'The ambivalence of psychoanalysis', p. 69, emphasis in original.
28. *The Good Society and the Inner World: psychoanalysis, politics and culture*, Verso, London, 1991, p. 55.
29. *The Repression of Psychoanalysis*, p. 66.
30. See Puget, J., 'Social violence and psychoanalysis in Argentina: the unthinkable and the unthought', *Free Associations*, No. 13, 1988.
31. Langer, M., *From Vienna to Managua: journey of a psychoanalyst*, Free Association Books, London, 1989, p. 110.

32. *Wild Desires and Mistaken Identities*: Lesbianism and psychoanalysis, Virago, London, 1993.
33. 'Culture in a democratic society', *The Castoriadis Reader* (Curtis, D. A. ed. and trans.), Blackwell, Oxford, 1997, pp. 132–3, 342.
34. All Castoriadis quotes in this section are from 'Psychoanalysis and politics', *World in Fragments: writings on politics, society, psychoanalysis and the imagination* (Curtis, D. A. ed. and trans.), Stanford University Press, Stanford, 1997.

Chapter 8

1. Merleau-Ponty, M., 'An unpublished text', *The Primacy of Perception* (trans. A. B. Dallery), Northwestern University Press, Evanston, 1964, p. 9.
2. *Finnegans Wake*, Faber and Faber, London, 1939, p. 114.
3. *The Wittgenstein Reader* (Kenny, A. ed.), Blackwell, Oxford, 1994, p. 257.
4. *Otherwise Than Being or Beyond Essence* (trans. A. Lingis), Martinus Nijhoff, Dordrecht, 1974, p. 170.
5. I am here indebted to the thinking of John Heaton. See for example his articles 'The sceptical tradition in psychotherapy', *From the Words of my Mouth: tradition in psychotherapy* (Spurling, L. ed.), Routledge, London, 1993, and 'Pyrrhonian scepticism: a therapeutic phenomenology', *Journal of the British Society for Phenomenology*, 28, 1997.
6. Nussbaum, M.C., *The Therapy of Desire: theory and practice in Hellenistic ethics*, Princeton University Press, Princeton, 1994, p. 315.
7. *The Therapy of Desire*, p. 15.
8. *The Therapy of Desire*, pp. 490–91.

9. *Outlines of Scepticism*, quoted in Heaton, J. M., 'Pyrrhonian scepticism: a therapeutic phenomenology' in *Journal of the British Society for Phenomenology*, 28, 1997.
10. Heaton, 'Pyrrhonian scepticism'.
11. Heaton, 'Pyrrhonian scepticism'.
12. 'On experience' quoted in Cooper, R., 'What we take for granted', *Free Associations*, Vol. 6, No. 4, 1997.
13. Evans, R. *R. D. Laing: the man and his ideas*, E. P. Dutton, New York, 1976, p. 90.
14. *Clinical Seminars and Other Works*, Karnac Books, London, 1994, p. 17.
15. 'Ethics as first philosophy', *The Levinas Reader* (Hand, S. ed), Blackwell, Oxford, 1989, p. 78.
16. 'The Dry Salvages', *Four Quartets*, Faber and Faber, London, 1944, p. 39.
17. 'East Coker', *Four Quartets*, p. 26.
18. 'East Coker', p. 26.
19. 'East Coker', pp. 26–7.
20. 'Friendship', *Essays*, 1841.
21. *Guardian*, 14 March 1998.

Permissions

The author and publishers gratefully acknowledge the following:

Anvil Press Poetry for permission to quote from 'Speak You, Also' from the *Poems of Paul Celan* translated by Michael Hamburger.

Carcanet Press Ltd for permission to quote from 'Persuasion' from *Sweeping Out the Dark* by Edwin Morgan; and 'Wanda' from *Facing the River* by Czeslaw Milosz.

The Estate of W. S. Graham for permission to quote from 'The Constructed Space' and 'Malcolm Mooney's Land' from *Selected Poems* and 'Kandinsky's Ribbons' from *Aimed at Nobody* by W. S. Graham.

Faber and Faber for permission to quote from 'Four Quartets' and 'Marina' from *Collected Poems 1909–1962* by T. S. Eliot; from 'Sketch of the Great Dejection' from *The Man With Night Sweats* by Thom Gunn; and 'Epilogue' from *Day by Day* by Robert Lowell; from 'Chocorua to its neighbour', 'On modern poetry' and 'Final soliloquy of the interior paramour' from *Collected Poems of Wallace Stevens*.

Yale University Press for permission to quote from 'Ashglory' by Paul Celan, translated by John Felstiner and published in *Paul Celan: poet, survivor, Jew* by John Felstiner.

185

Index

Ahmad, Aijaz, 141
ambiguity, 123, 124
anthropology, 142, 143
arrogance, 23–4, 42
asymmetry, 48, 51, 55
attention, 88–9, 97, 114
Auden, W. H., 103
authority, 55
autonomy, 151–3

Bachelard, Gaston, 45, 104, 110,
    113–14, 117, 118, 119, 126,
    129
Bakhtin, Mikhail, 45, 67–71, 73,
    76–7
Bauman, Zygmunt, 51, 55–6, 57
being, 49, 50
belonging, 104, 108
Bion, W. R., 22, 37, 38, 44, 89–90,
    91, 122, 140, 145, 158
Blanchot, Maurice, 86, 88–9, 94
Bohm, David, 80–81
British Psycho-Analytical Society,
    25
Brodsky, Joseph, 131
Buber, Martin, 48

caring, 21–2, 23, 58
Carver, Raymond, 19
Castoriadis, Cornelius, 10, 28, 42,
    43, 45, 119, 132, 137, 141,
    144–5, 151–3
Celan, Paul, 98, 100, 120, 121–2,
    123, 133–5

Cezanne, Paul, 12
Coleridge, Samuel, 93
Coltart, Nina, 23, 25
consciousness, 117
conversation, 35, 37, 39, 52, 63,
    65–6, 70, 77
    silence in, 78–80
    social context of, 76
    therapeutic, 80–5
    see also language
Cooper, David, 19, 31, 32
Cooper, Robin, 22, 109, 115, 158
counselling, 14, 23
creativity, 29, 67, 91, 92–3, 113,
    119, 125
criticism, 141
culture, understanding of,
    142–3

day-dreaming, 113, 126
democracy, 151–2, 153
determinism, 113
dialectic, 80–1
dialogism, 67–71
dialogue, 63, 80–1
    see also conversation; dialogism
discussion, 80
Doctorow, E. L., 99
doctors, 26, 30, 35, 70
domination, 140
    see also power
dreaming, 113–14
drugs, 32, 33

dwelling, 108, 113, 117
  see also home; house

ecological movements, 105
ego, 52, 152
Eisold, Kenneth, 25
Eitington, Max, 150
Eliot, T. S., 22, 92, 108, 120, 122,
  123–4, 127–8, 130, 135, 159,
  160, 161
Emerson, Ralph Waldo, 162
emotions, 20, 65, 69, 70, 76, 77,
  100–1
empathy, 57–8
encounter, 16, 46, 55–7, 81
ethics, 34, 46–62, 86, 137, 156,
  161, 162, 163
  codes of, 35–6, 57–8, 59
  and language, 59–62
  and poetry, 128–36
  and responsibility, 57–9
expression, 69, 72
  see also language; speech

face, the, 53–7, 59
Fanon, Frantz, 147
Felman, Shoshana, 98
Fenichel, Otto, 41, 140, 148–9,
  150
Feyerabend, Paul, 28
Fiumara, Gemma Corrada, 72, 74
Free Associations project, 41
Freud, Sigmund, 15, 19, 24, 25,
  26–7, 31, 37, 40, 41, 42, 56,
  70, 72, 77, 81, 113, 119, 139,
  142, 143, 150, 152, 153, 157
Friedman, Joe, 86–7
'friendship', 162–3
Fromm, Erich, 41, 149

Gadamer, Hans Georg, 73, 75
Gans, Steve, 53, 62
God, 91–2, 131
goodness, 58
Graham, W. S., 78. 126–7
Gray, Alasdair, 125
Gunn, Thom, 115–16

happiness, 43, 44
Heaney, Seamus, 120, 130, 131
Heaton, John, 62, 156, 157
Heidegger, Martin, 48, 66, 71, 73,
  103, 108, 124
Heller, Agnes, 79–80, 105–7, 114
Heraclitus, 155, 159
Hillman, James, 138–9
home, 104–17
'homelessness', 104, 108
homosexuality, 144, 151
hospitality, 107, 110, 111, 112,
  116, 135, 163
house, 109, 112, 114
  see also home; place
humility, 42, 161
humour, 22–3

Ibn, Arabi, 12
ideas, 45
Illich, Ivan, 33–4, 78–9
individuals, 68, 69, 70, 137, 138,
  139, 145, 151–3
Ingleby, David, 31, 142, 149
'inner world', 38–9
International Psycho-Analytical
  Association, 24, 25
interpretation, 83–4, 90, 91, 97,
  123
invitation, 111, 116, 135

Jacoby, Russell, 31, 41, 140, 147,
  148, 150
Jarrell, Randall, 132
Jones, Ernest, 24
Joyce, James, 37, 154
Jung, C., 40

Keats, John, 92–3, 158
Klein, Melanie, 24, 40, 41, 75,
  113, 140
knowledge, 14, 19, 20, 23, 24, 38,
  47–9, 55, 98, 158, 159,
  160–1
Kotowicz, Zbigniew, 113
Kovel, Joel, 140
Kurtz, Stephen, 90–1

Index

Lacan, Jacques, 24, 25, 140
Laing, R. D., 12, 24, 31, 32, 37,
    109, 158
Langer, Marie, 147–8, 150
language, 59–62, 100–1, 119, 121,
    122–3, 136
    and dialogism, 67–71
    and emotion, 76–7
    importance of, 63
    and silence, 78–80
    and the speaking subject, 64–7
    see also poetry
Lasch, Christopher, 145
Laub, Dori, 97–8
leaving, 115
'leaving be', 111
Lefebvre, Henri, 103
Levi, Primo, 95–7, 98
Levinas, Emmanuel, 14, 17, 45,
    46–62, 69, 73, 86, 107, 108,
    117, 134–5, 155, 159, 161,
    163
listening, 63–4, 67, 71–8, 114
    and silence, 79
    and speaking, 73
    and witnessing, 97–8
literature, 118, 119
    see also language; poetry
Lomas, Peter, 17, 22–3, 81–2
love, 66, 135
Lowell, Robert, 40

Magritte, René, 118
Mandelstam, Nadezhda, 131
Marquez, Gabriel Garcia, 99
Marxism, 140
meaning, 65, 66, 67, 76, 79, 153,
    158
medicine, 30–3, 34
mental illness, 32, 33
Meltzer, Donald, 38
Merleau-Ponty, Maurice, 14, 39,
    45, 64, 65, 66, 77, 104,
    124–5, 154
metaphor, 38–9, 104, 117, 118,
    119, 120
Mickiewicz, Adam, 9

Milosz, Czeslaw, 95
mind, 38, 64, 70
    see also thought
miners' strike of 1984/5, 145–6
Montaigne, Michel de, 14, 16
moralism, 20
Morgan, Edwin, 44, 129
music, modern, 88

Nagy, Ágnes Nemes, 100
naming, 99–102
'negative capability', 93, 126, 158,
    161
negative way, the, 91–3
Neruda, Pablo, 129
nuclear weapons, 144
Nussbaum, Martha, 156

Oakley, Chris, 39
objectivity, 27, 28, 29, 32
O'Connor, Noreen, 143, 151
Orbach, Susie, 36, 100
other, the, 37, 46, 47, 48, 49–50,
    54, 60, 62, 69, 75, 94, 133,
    134, 135, 159, 163
    hostage to, 57
    see also responsibility for the
        other

patience, 94, 110
patient, the, 87, 94, 97, 102, 111
personal relationships, 39, 46, 47,
    48, 52, 69–70
personal therapy, and politics,
    140–1
persons, 65, 68
Phillips, Adam, 162
Philadelphia Association, 109, 158
philosophy, 14, 25, 28, 45,
    46–8ff., 74, 153, 156
place, 110–14
    metaphorical, 104–10, 117
play, 113
pleasure, 43, 44–5
poetry, 61, 100, 118–36
    ethics of, 128–36
    process of, 124–8

social nature of, 130–1
postmodernism, 49, 104, 141
power, 20, 23–5, 83, 141
professionalism, 33–7
psychiatry, 31–3
psychoanalysis, 23, 24–5, 39, 45,
    70, 71, 77, 81, 113, 119, 138
  aim of, 152
  politics of, 139, 140–6, 148–51
  and scepticism, 157
  and science, 26–8
psychotherapy, 14
  and dangers of naming, 101–2
  dialogue in, 63, 80–5
  and double witnessing, 97–8
  and expression, 72
  and face to face encounter, 56–7
  and friendship, 162–3
  house or place of, 109–17
  and the individual, 68, 69
  and listening, 71–2, 75, 77
  medicalisation of, 30–3
  and the poetic process, 124–8
  politics of, 15–16, 41–2, 137–53
  and questioning, 80–1, 82
  regulation of, 34–6
  and responsibility for the other,
    52–3
  and sanctity, 21–3
  and sense of home, 109–17
  and status, 29
  and theory, 37–41, 48, 62, 69,
    75, 141, 157
  and witnessing, 97–8
  see also psychoanalysis; therapist

questioning, 80–1, 82, 111, 141,
    156, 157, 158, 163

racism, 143
radical therapy, 147–8
reciprocity, 47, 50, 163
Rée, Jonathan, 56
redress, 130
refuge, 109, 110
Reich, Wilhelm, 24, 41, 140, 150
religion, 21
response, 73, 77

responsibility for the other, 46, 47,
    48, 50–3, 54, 56, 58, 62, 163
  content of, 57–9
  meaning of, 58–9
'right to exist', 54
Różewicz, Tadeusz, 121
rules, 57, 59, 60
Rustin, Michael, 150
Ryan, Joanna, 143, 151
Rycroft, Charles, 24, 83, 84, 112

Sacks, Oliver, 33, 69–70
Samuels, Andrew, 142–3
St John of the Cross, 91, 92
Sartre, Jean Paul, 48
'saying' and 'said', 60–2
scepticism, 14, 41, 154–63
  meaning of, 156
  and truth, 155
Schneider, Monique, 77
Schwarz, Joe, 27
science, 26–30
Segal, Hanna, 26, 144
self, 52, 53, 56, 69, 133, 134
self-reflectiveness, 151–2
Serge, Victor, 95
setting, therapeutic, 111–13
sex, 36, 39, 143–4
sexual abuse, memories of, 17, 20
Sextus Empiricus, 156
silence, 77, 78–80, 97, 101, 126
Simic, Charles, 120, 124, 128–9,
    131, 132
Simmel, Ernst, 150
social context, 15–16, 41–2, 58,
    76, 137–53
social interaction, 67–8, 69–70,
    76
socialism, 139
Sontag, Susan, 39
South Africa, 148
spatiality, 103–4, 113
speech, 59, 63, 64–7, 69–71, 98,
    122
  and listening, 73, 76
  see also conversation; language
'stay among things', 108–9

Steiner, George, 65, 141
Stevens, Wallace, 63, 117, 120,
    121, 129, 131, 133
subjectivity, 47, 49, 51–2
suffering, 43, 53, 58, 77, 95, 97,
    156

Tavistock Clinic, 42
talking, 63, 71
    see also conversation; language;
    speech
Taylor, Charles, 65
testimony, 98
therapeia, meaning of, 86–7
therapeutic community, 109,
    115
therapist, 14
    anonymity of, 82
    and compulsion to make sense,
    90–1
    facing the other, 56–7
    legal responsibility of, 31, 36
    and listening, 71–2, 75
    passivity of, 93–4, 102
    and self-disclosure, 82–3
    training, 35, 36, 139
    and waiting, 86–8
    see also psychoanalysis;
    psychotherapy
thinking, 156, 160
thought, 64, 113, 156, 160
thoughtfulness, 40

tone, 76–7
transference, 90
truth, 28, 39, 45, 98, 132, 135,
    155, 161, 163

understanding, 49, 66, 73, 75, 90,
    91, 159, 161
unhappiness, 42–5
unknowing, 91–2, 160

Viola, Bill, 91–2

waiting, 102, 125, 126
    and attention, 88–9
    and patience, 94
    and unknowing, 91–3
    'waiting for', 87–8
Wajda, Andrzej, 77
war protests, 144
Webber, George, 115
Wenders, Wim, 88, 116, 125–6
Williams, William Carlos, 118, 121
Winnicott, D. W., 22–3, 84, 90,
    101
wisdom, 48, 159–61
witnessing, 95–8, 102
Wittgenstein, Ludwig, 27, 39, 64,
    77, 155
Wolfe, Thomas, 114–5
words *see* language; speech
world, the, 114, 115, 116, 117
writing, 66, 67